October 1998

Betty,
Enjoy the quilts!
Best wishes.

Judy Sickdon

FLOWERS *in* APPLIQUÉ

*Fast and Simple Quilting
with Printed-Motif Fabrics*

Judy Severson

THE QUILT DIGEST PRESS
NTC/Contemporary Publishing Group

Library of Congress Cataloging-in-Publication Data

Severson, Judy.
    Flowers in appliqué : fast and simple quilting with printed-motif fabrics /
  Judy Severson.
       p.   cm.
   ISBN 0-8442-2658-0
   1. Appliqué.   2. Quilting.   3. Flowers in art.
 TT779.S38   1998
 746.46—dc21   98-13134
                                                   CIP

To my parents, John and Ruby Ryman

Acknowledgments

This book could not possibly have been written without the help of many people, including the quilters of times past whose work continues to inspire us today. I am grateful to all of them. I would especially like to thank the many quilt researchers who continue to bring to light the wonderful quilts from the past, most notably: Joyce Gross, for sharing her time and collection and allowing me to travel with her in search of quilts from earlier decades and often earlier centuries; Cuesta Benberry, for sharing her collection and understanding of quilt history; Barbara Brackman, for her insightful research on appliqué and *broderie perse* here in the United States; and Dorothy Osler, for her quilt research in England.

    I also wish to thank my quilt teachers, Winnie McClelland, Lucy Hilty, Elly Sienkiewicz, and Susie Ernst, all of whom have given me good training.

    I am grateful to the friends who have either allowed me to use their quilts or otherwise helped me to make this book possible: Brenda Blackman, Bobbi Finley, Toni Fisher, Bettina Havig, Martha Noha, Becky Schaefer, Jeri Thomason, and Laurie Williams.

    My appreciation also to Alina Cowden, for her support and encouragement.

    I am indebted to Anne Knudsen, my editor, for understanding my idea for this book and making it a reality.

    Special thanks to my partner in business, Robin Whyte, for steadfastly believing in my work for the last 11 years and for helping me with this book, and to my partner in love, Peter, who gives balance to my life.

Editorial direction by Anne Knudsen
Project editing by Gerilee Hundt
Art direction by Kim Bartko
Cover design by Kim Bartko
Cover photograph by Sharon Risedorph
Interior design by Mary Lockwood
Illustrations by the author, digitally colorized by Mary Lockwood and Monica Baziuk
All interior photography by Sharon Risedorph, except page 78 (photograph by
Sharon Hoogstraten), unless otherwise credited

Published by The Quilt Digest Press
A division of NTC/Contemporary Publishing Group, Inc.
4255 West Touhy Avenue, Lincolnwood (Chicago), Illinois 60646-1975 U.S.A.
Printed in Singapore
International Standard Book Number: 0-8442-2658-0
18   17   16   15   14   13   12   11   10   9   8   7   6   5   4   3   2   1

Contents

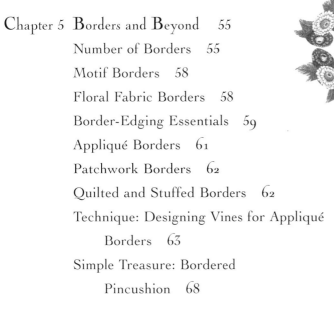

Evening Star, 102″ × 110″ (259cm × 279.4cm)
Designed and hand-stuffed by Judy Severson,
machine-quilted by Shirley Greenhoe

*D*ear *R*eader,

    *M*any years ago, on my visits to museums *I* started seeing the chintz quilts of the late seventeenth and early eighteenth centuries. *T*hese extraordinary quilts, with their beautiful flowers so artfully arranged, always seemed to speak to me. *I* still love their garlands and wreaths, which, although from an earlier time, would be perfect in many homes today.

    *W*hat *I* remembered from these early chintz quilts was that they used whole garlands and entire groups of flowers that showed off the beauty of the original printed fabric. *I*n later years, the term chintz quilts changed to broderie perse, and they usually were made by cutting out flowers one by one and stitching them onto the background fabric individually. *T*hese later quilts obviously required much more time and labor.

    *A*s *I* started to find larger floral and border print fabrics in quilt shops, *I* began to think about how *I* could use the early approach in my quilts. *I* studied how floral prints are designed and started looking at fabrics from different angles. *O*nce *I* discovered the garlands and bouquets that are readily available in today's fabrics, *I* learned that *I* could take advantage of the repeats and designs in the fabrics themselves to create my own quilts, inspired by chintz quilts from the past. *N*ow *I* would like to share my discovery with you.

    *M*y wish is that this book will give you a better understanding of floral fabrics, which you can use in creating elegant and romantic quilts. *I* hope you too will discover the joy and the simplicity of designing new quilts from floral printed motifs.

*W*ith warmest regards,

Judy Severson

one

Getting Started: Planting a Seed

Flowers are an enduring motif among quilters, particularly among those who appliqué. Quilters have always taken inspiration from the world around them and the flowers that grow in their gardens. Floral appliqué patterns have been handed down from quilter to quilter since colonial times. Floral fabrics are a part of every quilter's fabric collection and, through the ages, flowers have inspired the most popular designs for quilts of all kinds.

I call the quilts in this book *printed-motif quilts*. Reminiscent of Victorian elegance, floral quilts from printed motifs are deceptively simple to make. Unlike traditional appliqué, there are no tiny flowers or petals to work with nor delicate stems to stitch. Instead, you use larger groupings of flowers, bouquets, vines, or swaths, all cut from a single favorite fabric or a selection of fabrics. As you arrange and rearrange the pieces, the quilt takes shape and quickly progresses. As if by magic, you find that all the flowers blend together nicely since they come from the same fabric pieces.

Since the final look of the quilt depends upon the fabric you choose, I think making printed-motif quilts allows you to express your creativity more than any other type of quilt making. More-

Vintage Rose, 65″ × 72″ (165cm × 183cm)
Designed and hand-appliquéd by Judy Severson,
machine-quilted by Shirley Greenhoe

over, since there is no set pattern, all the quilts you make will be different, even if you do repeat some of the same fabrics. These quilts have a balance and symmetry to their design, yet they allow for individuality. My floral-motif quilts remind me of freshly picked flowers lying across my bed. Whether a single bloom, a beautiful bouquet, or a graceful garland, the flowers are always fresh and, year round, they remind me of springtime in my garden.

The recent introduction and the incredible range available of beautiful large-scale floral quilting fabrics mean that floral-motif quilts are a wonderful option for today's quilters. It is easy to find fabrics that will inspire you to begin. And the better you learn to read fabrics—finding secret bouquets, pretty twists of flowers, and intricate greenery—the more elaborate your quilts will become. Printed-motif quilts are appealing to the beginning quilter because they come together so quickly and because they teach a range of simple yet essential skills. They are also a breath of fresh air for the more experienced quilter. The techniques can easily be combined with patchwork, stuffed work, and other appliqué for more sophisticated effects.

Vintage Rose is one of the simplest printed-motif quilts I have made. The inspiration came from a piece of 1940s English chintz that was given to me by a special friend. It was beautiful—a mauve, pink, and red rose centered in a bouquet of blue, pink, and red flowers with a soft green background. For Vintage Rose I used a solid 14" (35cm) block of the vintage fabric, surrounded by five borders of complementary green calico fabrics. The fourth border contains an appliqué garland, with a vintage rose cut out and sewn to the top of the garland with two additional small leaves. The quilt was machine-quilted, but the appliqué was left unquilted to stand out.

Printed-Motif Appliqué

Appliqué is a quilt-making term for sewing a small piece of fabric onto a larger piece for a decorative effect. You can use fabric of any design or pattern in a conventional appliqué quilt. Traditionally, the fabric to be appliquéd is cut into a particular shape—such as a rose or a leaf—regardless of the design printed on the fabric itself.

In printed-motif appliqué, however, there is no need to cut and make those delicate shapes; they already exist as part of the fabric design. When you make a motif quilt, you simply cut out a design that is printed on your fabric, and sew that design onto the ground fabric of your quilt.

Because I'm a gardener as well as a quilter, my favorite cutouts are florals, which are the subject of this book. A floral appliqué motif can be constructed from one leaf, one flower, a group of flowers, or an entire basket filled with flowers. There is no set pattern or design. It is up to the individual quilter to use the printed fabrics she has chosen and to combine them into a design of her own.

Flower-on-Flower

Flower-on-flower is one way to create a motif quilt. You cut out and arrange individual flowers, buds, petals, and leaves on the ground fabric and then appliqué them one by one to form a new design, perhaps a wreath or a bouquet. Though flower-on-flower takes time and care, with each piece stitched separately, the results are quite sensational.

Flower Groups

An equally beautiful option, one that is much simpler and less time-consuming, is to select and cut groups of flowers and leaves to be used as a motif. The border of *Blue Garland* is made in this way (see page 16). Though you are naturally more dependent on the fabrics you choose, this method goes much more quickly. Once these larger floral motifs are combined with borders of patchwork,

Flowers in Appliqué

stuffed work, or other appliqué, the quilt takes on a look all its own, which, though simple, seems elaborate.

How to Use Flowers in Appliqué

Each chapter of this book opens with a printed-motif quilt. In the first quilt, at the beginning of this chapter, it is easy for the novice to see how to make a uniquely personal quilt just by adding a few flowers to a simple border. As you progress through the book, the quilts have additional printed motifs to inspire you. The Quilt Patterns section provides drawings that reveal exactly how each of these quilts was constructed. You can use these as patterns for your own quilts. Each chapter also includes a technique section that focuses on a particular skill required to make the quilt featured in that chapter. With an emphasis on simplicity, these sections cover all the essentials of appliqué and patchwork. They help you create the quilt top, put the quilt together, and embellish it in a variety of ways. In addition to the full-quilt projects, most of the chapters offer what I call a Simple Treasure—a smaller project that can be completed in a matter of just a few hours. These simple treasures make delightful gifts as well as lovely personal items.

Quilter's Creativity

A successful floral-motif quilt has a balance and rhythm, drawing the eye in and around it. You achieve this balance through your choice of colors and fabrics and your selection and arrangement of motifs.

The complexity and interest of motifs depends solely on the imagination of the quilter, so take your time selecting and combining your fabrics. One piece of floral fabric can be cut up and sewn onto a ground to make an entire quilt, but it will not be as interesting or as creative as one made of multiple printed-motif fabrics. In the most intricate quilts, the design might even look as though it was preprinted on the fabric.

There are several simple techniques you can use to add extra interest to your quilts. Some of the prettiest floral quilts use borders that complement the center motif design. It is easy to enhance your design by repeating a fabric from the body of the quilt in the border, as in all the quilts featured in Chapters 1 through 7. Once the top of the quilt is completed, you can, if you wish, add stuffing to flowers or feathers in the quilt top, giving the quilt extra dimension. The batting is then sandwiched between the back and the floral quilt top.

Medallion quilt

Quilt Styles

The motif quilts in this book are created in one of three different styles—medallion, block, or framed. In a medallion quilt, the center block can be a square or a rectangle, with borders added until the quilt has reached its finished size. Or the center block can be a square set on point with additional borders. A block-style quilt can be four or more blocks sewn together, with or without sashes, and usually finished with a single border. A framed quilt contains a very large central body made up of a single piece of fabric (or two pieces of fabric joined together and used as a single piece of fabric), which is the ground for the motifs and other appliqué. The large center is framed with a border on the outside.

Square on point with borders

Technique: Printed-Motif Appliqué
Choosing Fabrics

Selecting a floral cutout can be as simple as choosing one flower from a floral fabric and then cutting it out, leaving a $3/16$" (0.5cm) seam allowance around the flower.

When you select a group of flowers for your motif, there are several things you should keep in mind. If the color of the ground is different from the color of the motif's background, the background will retain a certain prominence and the flowers will appear to be caught in a garland or ribbon. On page 16 you will see that my first motif quilt, *Blue Garland*, was fashioned this way because I saw blue garlands in the fabric. If I had decided to use the same color blue ground as the background of the cutout fabric, the back-

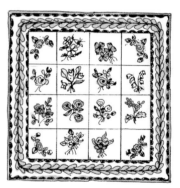

Block-style quilt

Framed quilt

Flowers in Appliqué

ground would have receded and the flowers would appear to be free and not trapped in a garland.

If you want your flowers to be prominent, choose a cutout whose background is the same color as the ground fabric. It will make your job slightly less difficult because you will not have to eliminate the contrasting background areas when making your motifs.

Try selecting a group of flowers to cut out. You will need to cut off the leaves that disappear behind flowers that you are not planning to include. Cut off all stems and flowers that are too small to appliqué around. Avoid including flowers from other groupings that may touch your selected group.

Now consider the overall shape of the motif. Is it a pleasing shape? Will it fill the area in which you wish to use it? Is it best to select a larger group of flowers and cut it down to size?

In the second fabric shown here, more care needs to be taken because the background of the fabric is a light blue. It is best not to leave any background showing between the leaves and flowers. The flowers then become part of the ground of the fabric and seem to open up.

The quilts and projects in this book can be made either by hand appliqué or by machine appliqué. Each method has its own set of advantages.

Hand Appliqué

The supplies you need for hand appliqué are simple: number 9 or number 10 sharp needles and a thimble. Alternatively, use number 9 to number 10 milliners needles that can be used without a thimble. Use all-cotton thread in a color close to the motif you are to appliqué.

Traditionally, appliqué was hand-stitched using a tack stitch and a needle-turning technique to turn the edges under. This technique leaves the motif soft and as supple as the original fabrics, but the hand stitching takes a little time. I was lucky to learn from a gifted quilter and family friend, Winnie McClelland. Her method has served me well. She felt that you should appliqué while sitting relaxed in a comfortable chair. In your lap you should have a light-weight board or strong piece of cardboard covered with contact or shelf paper. Your quilt should lie across the board to remain smooth while being stitched. Appliqué should be relaxing and should leave you free to talk or watch television.

Tying a Knot

Thread your needle, pulling the thread about 2″ (5cm) shorter on one end than on the other. Take the end in your left hand, with the needle pointing up in your right. Wrap the thread three times around tightly over itself and hold the part you wound with your left hand (assuming you are right-handed). Push the needle up through the wound part and pull to the bottom of the thread. There should be a small knot. It may take you several tries. The size of the knot will be determined by how many times you wrap the thread around the needle.

Making the Stitch

Place the motif on the ground. A washable glue stick applied to the underside or a safety pin will hold it temporarily in place. The tack stitch is the most invisible stitch used for appliqué. The buttonhole stitch or the outline stitch, which are decorative stitches, can also be used (see page 123). Either way, short small stitches are important. Using your finger or the top of your needle, fold the edge of the motif under the edge of the flower. Bring the needle up through the ground, just catching the edge of the motif, with the knot on the underside. Pull the thread up through the fabric and then push the needle down through the ground directly opposite where the needle came through the motif. Move the needle ahead about ¼″ (0.75cm), again catching the edge of the motif. Repeat. Use the point of your needle to turn under the outside edge of the flower. Inside curves need to be clipped almost to the fold line before turning under. Sharp points should be clipped.

To increase accuracy and speed up hand appliqué a little, try using fusible web. See the following section on machine appliqué for an explanation of this. Fusible web is particularly useful for

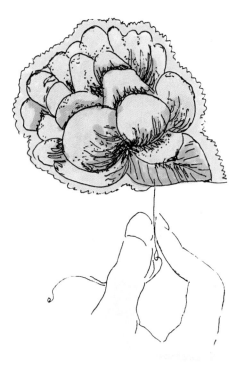

small or complex motifs, as it helps stabilize the fabric while you stitch.

Machine Appliqué

Much quicker than hand stitching, machine appliqué is easier still if you use fusible web (glue on a web, fashioned so it can be ironed, causing two fabrics to adhere to each other). Usually it is simply ironed onto the backs of the motifs and then trimmed to their shape. The motifs are positioned on the ground fabric, ironed, and then the edges are machine-stitched. This method leaves the motif with a slight stiffness from the fusible web, but this process makes the work go more quickly. Some people fear, however, that the webbing may over a period of time cause the fabrics to weaken.

For machine appliqué, you will need fusible web (such as Steam-a-Seam) a little larger than your printed motif, an iron, scissors, a pressing cloth, an embroidery foot for the sewing machine, and a square coffee filter to fit under the motif to allow the sewing machine to move freely.

To prepare the fusible web, heat your iron to the cotton setting. Peel off the printed liner of the fusible web, place it on top of the motif and trace the design. Cut the web to shape. Place the web on the wrong side of the motif, leaving the second liner attached to the web, and press the right side with your iron. Peel off the second liner of web and place the motif on the ground where desired. Cover the fusing with a damp press cloth. Press for 10 seconds using steam. Always follow the directions shown on the fusible web package. If you want your motifs to overlap, trim away most of what would be covered by another motif. You need only a slight overlap so that the fabric will not become stiff.

Open the coffee filter flat and place it under the fused motif. Using your embroidery foot, machine-stitch the edges by outlining the motif with a straight stitch or satin stitch. Once completed, tear off the filter from the underside of the motif. If you prefer, you can use a hand buttonhole stitch to embellish your motif (see page 121). You will not need the filter if you're hand-stitching.

Simple Treasure Bag for Pearls

My mother gave me my first string of pearls when I turned 21. They came in a small silk bag and were forever falling out of it. Knowing how easily pearls scratch, I wanted to create a special bag that was easy to use. This bag is made of floral fabric on the outside, with hand-dyed cotton inside. I cut a single rose with leaves and used fusible web to attach it to the inside edge of the bag. I outlined the rose petals and leaves with gold thread. On the outside edge where the two fabrics are stitched together, I added a small gold cord that I blanket-stitched along the edge. The bag is tied with a medium elastic cord so that the bow does not need to be tied and untied every time I use the pearls.

Instructions

1. With a compass, draw a 12″ (30cm) circle on your paper. Cut the circle out, fold it in half, and cut along the fold line.

2. Draw the two half circles on the wrong side of fabric that will be the bag, leaving ¼″ (0.75cm) all around.

3. Cut out the two halves of the bag, ¼″ (0.75cm) from the drawn line.

4. Place the right sides together. Pin along the center line with the first pin ¼″ (0.75cm) from the edge of the circle. Measure 2″ (5cm) from the first pin and pin at that point. Place the next pin ½″ (1.3cm) below that pin and then place additional pins as needed down the middle line.

5. Starting at edge of the fabric, stitch the center line to the 2¼″ (5.5cm) pin and backstitch. Leave the next ½″ (1.3cm) open. Start stitching a few stitches and backstitch from that 2¾″ (7cm) pin and continue across the center to the other edge. Press seam. Check to see that you've left a ½″ (1.3cm) hole for the cord.

6. Using your pattern of half of a 12″ (30cm) circle, draw the pattern on the wrong side of the fabric for the bag's lining.

7. Place right sides together. Pin along the center line, starting at the outside edge. Measuring about 4″ (10cm) down from edge, place a pin. Measure another 4″ (10cm), then pin at the edge of the circle.

8. Starting at the top edge, stitch along the line to the 4″ (10cm) pin and then backstitch. Move the needle to the next pin, start stitching, backstitch, then continue to edge. This opening will allow you to turn the bag right-side out when it's been sewn together. Press the seam open.

Compass

Heavy paper

Ruler

Paper and fabric scissors

Pencil and tailor's chalk

2 compatible fabrics for
   outside and inside of bag,
   ½ yard (0.5 meter) each

Elastic cord, 1 yard
   (0.9 meter)

Straight pins

One safety pin

Fusible web (optional)

Embroidery thread and beads
   (optional)

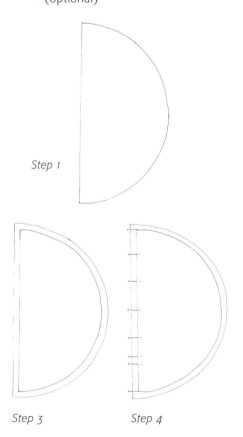

Step 1

Step 3   *Step 4*

Flowers in Appliqué

Step 5

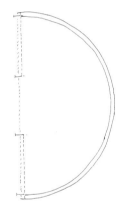

Step 7

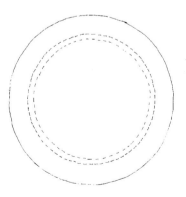

Step 11

9. Place the right sides of the bag and lining together and pin around the circle, checking to make sure the two edges line up. Stitch around the bag.

10. Using the opening in the lining, open the bag to the right side. Use a pin or toothpick to help make the circle smooth. Press.

11. Using your compass and paper, draw a 10" (25cm) circle and cut it out. Center the circle on the outside of the bag. Once it is centered, draw the circle with a tailor's chalk.

12. Either using that circle or another piece of paper, draw a circle 9½" (24cm) in diameter. Center it on the bag and draw a chalk line around the circle. Now check where the opening along the center stitching line is. It should be centered between your two chalk lines. If the placement is correct, stitch both circles in thread that is compatible with the fabric.

13. If you wish to choose a single flower from your outside fabric to add to the inside edge of the bag, select a small one. (See page 9 for help on using fusible web.)

14. The flower can now be embellished with stitches or beads. Additional stitching, such as blanket stitch, can be added to the top edge.

15. With 18" (46cm) cord or ribbon, tie a small knot at one end. Using the safety pin, pin through knot and close up the pin. Slide the pin through the opening on the right side and work it around the bag and bring pin and cord out the opening. Pull to gather the bag closed. Tie the elastic cord in a bow.

two

Reading Floral Fabrics

One day, as if by magic, I started finding whole bouquets of roses in some of my floral fabrics and springlike garlands in others. I could not believe my eyes at first, and I put the fabrics away. But I came back to them and, with encouragement from my quilt friends, I made my first floral-motif quilt. And then I made another.

I wanted to know why I could find those complete bouquets and garlands in some fabrics and not in others. I found the answers in *Textile Design* by Carol Joyce. This book taught me a great deal about how textiles are designed. With that new understanding, I can now look at a floral fabric and see its potential.

Fabric designs are constantly changing. They are continually influenced by everything around us—political, social, and economic. For example, in response to the modern interest in ecology, we find more landscapes, trees, and greens or other earth tones being used in current fabrics. When cows or frogs seem to be the rage, they show up in fabrics too.

Let's consider the many types of floral fabrics you can use in a printed-motif quilt. We'll discuss the variety of floral prints that

Blue Garland, 92″ × 92″ (234cm × 234cm)
Designed, hand-stuffed, and
hand-quilted by Judy Severson

exist, and then learn the different layouts that a textile designer can use to create fabric. Some of the layouts are more obvious than others. But by understanding the layout of fabric designs, you will be able to use the designs to their best advantage, like finding whole bouquets or garlands in some fabrics. You will also be taking advantage of what the fabric designers have already created. This bounty is just waiting for you at your local quilt shop!

Blue Garland was the first printed-motif quilt I ever made. I'd had the large blue floral fabric for several years and was hoping to hear of a class on motifs. I had been saving pictures of chintz quilts from the past and had at least 75 photos, many of them with floral garlands. From time to time I like to lay out fabrics from my collection and dream of how they could be made into quilts. While glancing at the blue floral one afternoon, I thought I saw a whole garland printed right in that fabric. Finally, at a class on chintz patchwork quilts taught by Barbara Brackman, I had the opportunity to talk to this wonderful teacher about chintz appliqué. With Barbara's encouragement and some experimentation, I was able to put the floral-motif quilt together. It just goes to show that sometimes you simply have to make a start on what you want to do and see what happens. Usually something good will result.

Floral Designs

Here are some designs to consider when you look for floral fabrics for your motif quilt.

- *Floral.* Multicolored flower prints are always the first thought for fabric when you're making a floral quilt. You will find the greatest selection and variety in this category. Flowers range from realistic to abstract to stylized.

- *Monotone.* These designs use only one color with white; for example, blue motifs on a white background. The absence of all but one color makes it easy to combine with other floral fabrics, but a monotone fabric can also be used alone.

- *Conversational.* A conversational design is a design with realistic or stylized motifs that either tell a story or contain a message. You might not pick these fabrics out of a crowd, but when you look closely there could be a stripe of flowers or a group of butterflies that would be just right for your quilt.

- *Paisley.* The paisley design is taken from cashmere shawls woven in Paisley, Scotland. Paisley designs are sometimes set and conservative, but can also be bold and dramatic. If the color is right, paisley can make an interesting motif for a quilt.

- *Border Stripe.* Stripes of continuous flowers that cross the width of the fabric, varying from ¼" to 1" (0.75cm to 2.5cm). They can be used as single or multiple stripes in a border or as sashing in a block-style motif quilt. Some of these fabrics were designed for impressionistic or watercolor quilts but should be considered for motif quilts as well.

- *Toile de Jouy.* The original textiles from the French town of Jouy depicted finely illustrated stories of current events as well as romanticized landscapes and figures. Contemporary toile designs are composed of pictorial or scenic motifs. Fabric designers once produced toiles only in heavier fabrics for home decorating, but

Floral

Monotone

Conversational

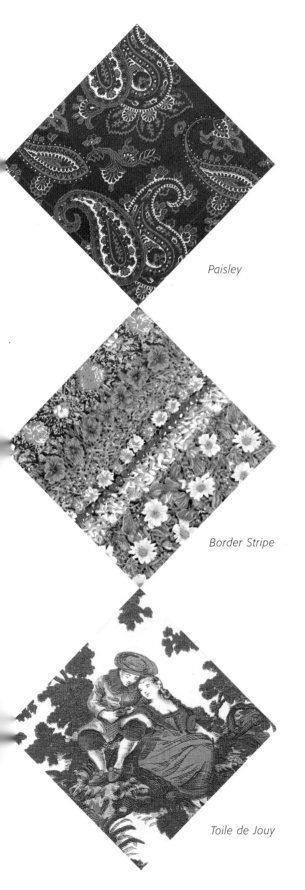

Paisley

Border Stripe

Toile de Jouy

lighter cotton toiles are made for quilters today. Toiles make a wonderful central medallion or can be used as a motif for a border.

Fabric Layout

Understanding the layout of textile designs will give you a better understanding of how these designs can be used. By the term *layout*, I refer to the arrangement of the design. When using a small design such as a calico, it is not so critical to know the arrangement. Calico is too small to use as a motif, although you might include a calico in the patchwork or conventional appliqué sections of your quilt. When you use a medium to large floral print in motif quilts, however, you can see all the different ways the floral print can be used if you know the layout and can recognize the pattern's repetitions.

If you are only going to cut out each flower and use it in a flower-on-flower arrangement, you might want to skip ahead to Chapter 3. However, if you want to find bouquets and hidden garlands in your fabrics, read on.

Directional and Nondirectional Fabric

Before starting on the layout, a fabric designer must decide whether it will be a one-way or two-way layout. In a one-way layout, the motifs face in the same direction. In a two-way layout, the motifs are positioned in two or more directions, so that when the fabric is turned around or upside down, there is no discernible difference. Most fabrics are done in a two-way or nondirectional layout.

When you first look at a fabric, see if there is a direction to the flowers. If there is no single direction, you will be able to use the fabric in any direction. Since your motifs are being appliquéd onto a ground, there is no need to consider the grain of the fabric as you would if you were cutting patchwork pieces.

Types of Layouts

There are nine types of layouts that are most commonly used in textile design: all-over or tossed, free-flowing, stripe, border, five-star, set, scenic or landscape, handkerchief square, and patchwork. I will not include the last four, because they are not important in a printed-motif quilt.

All-Over or Tossed

An all-over or tossed design is one in which the motifs are arranged in a variety of positions to achieve a balanced effect. The area that the motif covers on the background can range from packed, where the motifs are placed very close together, to spaced, which shows a lot of background.

All-over fabrics that contain packed floral motifs (with not much background) will give you a great many choices in finding your printed motif. They can be cut out as a single flower, or you can find larger units that even look like different types of bouquets or possibly garlands.

Later in this chapter, I will help you find the garlands in your fabric. These garlands can be used in the center of your medallion or in one of its borders. They can be cut in sections to curve in a circle or an oval. I created *Ring of Roses* in this way (see page 113).

Free-Flowing

A free-flowing layout, also known as pattern-on-pattern, uses an unconventional or asymmetrical layout with lots of flow and movement, like roses on a stripe. There is still a sense of balance with this design. Individual units can be cut out from this type of layout design for use in your quilt, but you must take extra care while you are cutting them from the background design. You do not want a different background from your ground, the fabric you are appliquéing to.

Stripe

A stripe layout is carefully planned and measured. Some stripes are easily recognizable as such, especially if there are lines defin-

All-Over

Packed

Spaced

All-Over Packed

Cut-Out Motif

Free-Flowing

Flowers in Appliqué

Small Stripe

Free-Flowing Stripe

Free-Flowing Stripe

Stripe Cutouts

Border Layout

Five-Star

ing them. Small stripes can combine with other stripes or be used on either side of an all-over design to make beautiful borders. Other stripes that are free-flowing, loose, or even those that seem to go into the next line are sometimes not easily recognizable as such. All floral stripes make excellent borders by themselves.

With a free-flowing stripe, you will have other choices. If the fabric has a large floral pattern, it can be cut into units to be used by themselves or combined with other motifs. I used these units with other flowers to make a bouquet as seen in *Flowers A-Bloom* (see page 42). The free-flowing stripe can be left in position, but cut so it can be curved into a circle or oval. You can then use it for a center of a medallion or in a large circle in a floral framed quilt. I used these types of floral units to form a large circle in *Belvedere Garden* (see page 122).

Border

A border layout is one that includes a border placed on one or both ends of a design. When placed on both ends of a design, a border layout may use either two of the same border or two different ones. The remainder of the printed fabric above the border is called the field. This layout gives you two fabrics in one. You can choose to use the border as a whole border on your quilt, and use the field as you would an all-over floral layout.

Five-Star

A five-star layout, also called a center bouquet, generally uses one central motif, often a large traditional bouquet. This central motif can be used as a whole motif or cut into smaller motifs. A five-star layout also makes for excellent borders as well, as in *Summer Flowers* (see page 94). You can use the bouquets as they are, cutting away any small flowers or leaves that are too small to appliqué. These are self-contained units that you can balance with each other or with other similar motifs in a formal, carefully thought out design. You might make the design circular or a balanced square. You can also use single, double, or up-and-down patterns.

Finding Hidden Garlands in Fabric

Garlands are found in floral fabrics in which the layout is packed with all-over design elements. Most garlands can be located by looking at the fabric on the bias, but at times they can be found running down the length of the fabric. Use the template pattern provided to cut two templates out of template plastic or heavy paper. Discard the center section.

Select one flower that will be the top of a garland and then find its repeat. Do this by turning the fabric at a 45° angle. If this is a packed all-over fabric, you will see the same flower repeated at least three times across the fabric on the bias.

Use the template so the open ends are facing each other. Place the template around the flower that is to be the top of the garland. The template is roughly the shape of a garland, and the template will help train your eye to find a garland in your fabric. This template might be too small for oversized fabrics and too large for some medium floral motifs, but it will give you a start in finding the hidden garlands.

Look at several different flowers that you might want to use for the top of the garland. What you are looking for in the garland are flowers that seem to flow out of each other, showing little or no background between the flowers. Sometimes you will have a choice of flowers to be at the top of the garland, and other times only one flower will work. Your garland does not have to be perfectly symmetrical because flowers do not grow that way. It may take time to train your eye to find the garlands, but the more you try, the more often you will find them.

Garlands are perfect in floral-motif quilts. Since the flowers are all cut out of one solid piece of fabric, they are a breeze to appliqué. You only have to turn the outside edges of the garland under, not appliqué every flower individually. You know the flowers all go together because they were designed that way by a fabric designer. Look for other examples of this type of garland in *Blue Garland* (see page 16), *Rose Wreath* (see page 30), *Blue Rose* (see page 80) and *Ring of Roses* (see page 106).

Template–cut two

Lay cut-out template on top

Floral garland

Flowers in Appliqué

Evening Star–medallion

Evening Star–motifs with stars

Evening Star–star border

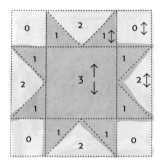

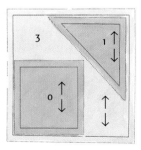

Technique: Patchwork Essentials

Simple patchwork blends well with motifs in a quilt, whether it is in the medallion, blocks, or borders. Using patchwork can add extra sparkle to the motifs, frame the motifs, and help make the quilt larger.

Most patchwork in motif quilts consists of squares and triangles. With today's modern equipment, it's easy to create exact piecing. The basic tools you will need are a rotary cutter, cutting mat, $6'' \times 24''$ (15cm × 60cm) heavy plastic ruler designed for use with the rotary cutter, pins, scissors, and a sewing machine with a $\frac{1}{4}''$ (0.75cm) wide presser foot.

In Chapter 5, I will discuss a variety of patchwork borders that you might want to use in your motif quilt. Here, however, I will tell you how to sew *Evening Star* (see page vi), just to cover the basics of how to put patchwork together. This pattern can be used as the medallion in your quilt, as a block alternating with motif blocks, or as stars in a border.

The block can be made to any size. The larger the pattern in the fabric, the larger the block should be to show off the fabric. The block used in my quilt is 10'' (25cm). This means the unfinished block would be $10\frac{1}{2}''$ (26cm) when you include the seam allowances.

Using your ruler and rotary cutter, cut the pieces accurately. Always cut away from your body. Arrows on the pattern show the direction of the grain of fabric. The grain means the lengthwise and crosswise threads in woven fabric.

Lay the pieces out in order. Set your machine at 15 stitches per inch (5.5 stitches per cm). Pin the smallest pieces together perpendicular to your seam. Sew with a $\frac{1}{4}''$ (0.75cm) seam allowance, using your presser foot as a guide. Pin the pieces in rows and sew. Pin seams together and sew the rows.

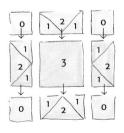

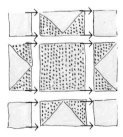

Reading Floral Fabrics

Simple Treasure

Scissors Fob

A scissors fob makes a lovely and useful gift for anyone who sews. I also hang one on the doorknob of my guest room and in other handy places throughout the house. I use one, too, for my folding travel scissors. I keep them in my pocket with the flower fob peeking out so I can find them easily. Other travelers often comment on it, thinking it a piece of jewelry. For this fob I used a flower design to which I could add interesting stitches and beads.

Instructions

1. Choose a flower in your fabric and cut a 3" (7.5cm) square around it.

2. Cut a square of fusible web smaller than your 3" (7.5cm) square. Tear off one side of the paper protecting the fusible web. Place the flower square on top of the web, lining it up square. Press the flower fabric to the web, using a cotton setting with no steam.

3. Cut the flower out to its finished shape.

4. Cut out three 4" (10cm) squares of ground fabric.

5. Pull off the paper from the fusible web and center the web on your ground fabric. Press the web onto the fabric to attach it.

6. You can embellish the flower with needlework or beading, or trim it with edging braid.

7. To stabilize the embellishment, cut another piece of fusible web smaller than the 4" (10cm) square ground with flower. Fuse the web to the back side of the embellished flower. Using a second square of ground fabric, fuse it to the flower to add stiffness to the scissors fob. Place a pencil mark on the edge of the square to show where the ribbon or cord will be.

8. Using a compass, draw a circle on your third piece of ground fabric. Make the circle ½" (1.3cm) larger than the flower.

9. Center the ground circle with right sides together on top of the flower. Pin around the circle, leaving ½" (1.3cm) on either side of the circle as your mark for the ribbon or cord to come out.

Supplies

Embroidery scissors or travel scissors

24" (60cm) of ¼" (0.75cm) ribbon or cord

Floral fabric with about 1½" to 2" (4cm to 5cm) flowers

¼ yard (0.25 meter) coordinating fabric for the ground

Fusible web

Compass

Small piece of cotton batt

Embroidery thread and beads (optional)

10. Stitch the circle to the flower square, leaving a 1" (2.5cm) opening at the top. Check to see if your circle is perfectly round; if not, adjust as necessary. Trim the circle and the square to ¼" (0.75cm) from the stitching line and clip.

11. Turn right sides out, pressing the seams open with the eraser end of a pencil or with the blunt end of a chopstick to make them smooth.

12. Cut a circle of cotton batt that is smaller than the fob and place the batt inside the fob.

13. Sew the fob closed, with a 10" (25cm) ribbon or cord folded in half, tucking the two ends inside the circle. You can add extra stitching or edging to the outside edge.

14. Attach the scissors by placing the folded end of the cord or ribbon through the handle. Push the fob through the folded end of the cord or ribbon and pull to secure. You can also add a bow or bead where the cord or ribbon is attached.

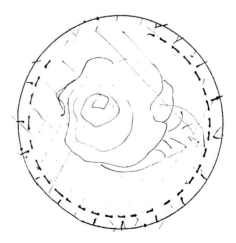

Right edges together, leaving top open for ribbon or cord, clip edges.

Reading Floral Fabrics

three

Choosing Fabrics

Choosing and buying fabric for a quilt is always exciting. Burrowing through the bolts of crisp new cottons, looking for just the right one . . . you never know where you will find that special floral fabric that will send you off into your next quilt.

Your choice of fabrics is very important to the construction of a printed-motif quilt. In most quilts you start with a template or pattern, and you cut the fabric to fit that design, whether patchwork or conventional appliqué. You're more concerned about the colors of the fabric than the printed motifs in the fabric. However, in motif quilts the patterns you cut out of your fabrics *are* the design, so the choice of fabrics is especially important, as discussed in Chapter 2.

All-Cotton Fabric

Although these quilts are based on chintz quilts from the past, the cotton chintz fabrics found in home-decorating stores today are tightly woven and are too stiff to quilt. They are very hard to needle when you appliqué and almost impossible to stitch with small stitches when you are doing your final quilting through the batt and backing. Also, print fabrics made with polyester are not a good

Rose Wreath, 94" × 93" (239cm × 236cm)
Designed and hand-stuffed by Judy Severson,
hand-quilted by Brenda Blackman

choice for a motif quilt. The problem with polyester is that it does not hold a crease, which makes it more difficult to appliqué.

The good news is that fabric companies are creating more all-cotton medium- and large-floral fabrics for quilters today. Pure cotton remains the best fabric choice for quilts.

There are three distinct elements for you to keep in mind when you choose your fabric: the printed motifs, the ground, and the borders.

Printed Motifs

First let's consider the fabric you'll need for the printed motifs used in the quilt. A medium- to large-floral print fabric is easiest to use. Most of the fabrics in printed-motif quilts are floral. The more floral fabrics you find that go well together, the more design choices you will have. Other motif fabrics you can use with the florals include butterflies, birds, fruit, and other flora or fauna.

This is the second quilt I made using floral motifs. I had just finished the first top and wanted to know if I could find the garlands again. Going through my fabric collection, I found another fabric with garlands. I pulled out other fabrics that might go into a new quilt and laid them out on a banister for a week. I used some of the same fabrics that I had used in Blue Garland in this quilt as well—bits of the toile in one border and some of the small border fabrics. I cut the outside floral garland first, and found there were roses and tulips left from that garland. I made a wreath for the center out of the roses. Then I sewed the tulips together to fill the triangles. I am always surprised by how these quilts end up looking antique—even when I am not trying to make them that way.

When you start a motif quilt, begin by choosing one floral fabric that you love, and then choose all the other fabrics to go with it. The scale of the motif fabrics doesn't need to be the same. Against larger and stronger-colored flowers, smaller patterns often provide a refreshing change of scale.

A quilt made with one fabric will not be as interesting as one with several different fabrics. If you can find only one motif fabric you particularly like, the quilt will be more interesting if you combine that fabric with other conventional appliqué or patchwork. Remember, it is important that the colors work well together.

Choose one floral fabric that will be dominant in your quilt. The more colors in the fabric, the easier it will be to find other motif fabrics to use with it. Not all the floral fabrics need to be multicolored. Simple one- or two-color prints on a white or off-white background can work well together and often serve to lighten multicolored fabrics. Monochromatic motif quilts too can be stunning.

Ground Fabric

If you look at the chintz quilts of the past, you'll see that they usually have white or off-white grounds, usually a simple muslin.

Today you have other choices when you select your ground. The key is to use a ground fabric that enhances the floral prints, rather than takes away from them.

Blend with Motif Background

First, start by looking at the background of the dominant floral fabric you are going to use. Is there a lot of background behind the flowers? How much background will show? If the background of the printed motif will show, choose a ground that is close to the background color of the floral print. Look at this blue background and ground as an example. Your flowers will seem to float free in the block or border if the ground and background are similar colors. The same flowers will be trapped inside the background of the floral fabric if you choose white or any other color ground. However, this might be the look you want; if so, then choose any color.

Flowers in Appliqué

Having the same color background and ground makes it easier to hide your quilting stitches. Also, when you stitch around a group of flowers, you will be able to leave more of the background between flowers. This will make your appliqué easier and faster.

If you are cutting out each flower and leaf and no ground will show, then your choice of ground color will not be important.

White or Off-White

The choice of a white or off-white ground allows all of the colors of your motifs to show up equally. For example, placing a red rose on a red fabric will make the flower blend in. If the red rose is on a white ground, it will stand out. White (or off-white) is also the best color for showing off stuffed work, trapunto, and quilting.

Tone-on-Tone

Another option is to select a ground fabric that has a small, light tone-on-tone print. A printed ground can add texture to your quilt. However, the busier the colors and the larger the pattern of the ground, the less you will see of the motifs. When using a subtle print for your ground, choose the pattern carefully.

Border Fabric

The last element that you need to consider is the fabric for your borders. The number of borders you add depends on which type of motif quilt you are planning to make as well as what types of borders you'd like to use. We will discuss borders in depth in Chapter 5, but here is a summary of the different types.

Motif Borders

You can use the same motif or motifs that you use in the medallion or blocks to form your border. You can also use whole floral garlands from one fabric, or you can form a garland from several different motifs. You might also consider combining motifs with other appliqué, such as vines and leaves. You can line up your motifs across the border or you can stagger them. However you place them, be sure that the four borders are balanced.

Floral Fabric Borders

You might decide to use one piece of fabric for your borders, such as a floral print—perhaps a print that you plan to use for one of your motifs or another print that harmonizes with your motifs. Fabrics that have a layout of a loose floral stripe or a five-star pattern are a good choice for borders.

You can also use a border print, which is fabric that has been designed specifically for use as a border. Border prints are readily available now at most quilt stores, and are becoming more popular. You can use the larger border prints as is. You might select other, smaller border prints (one to two inches wide) for use alone on the outside edge of a border. Think about combining a small border print with another wider piece of fabric to form a larger border. The fabric you use within this frame can be one of your floral motifs, a different floral, or a calico to accent the motif colors.

Besides using small border prints or framed borders, you can achieve the same finished effect with dogteeth, scallops, or other border-edging patterns. These are made with small to large floral patterns, as well as with a solid fabric.

Appliqué Borders

Appliqué borders of vines with leaves, flowers, and fruit such as grapes make interesting borders. I also like borders with swags or bows for accenting or blending colors.

Patchwork Borders

A simple patchwork border is often a very effective choice. The smaller the patchwork design, the smaller your floral pattern can be. When you choose larger floral fabrics, show off the fabric by working with a larger patchwork design.

Quilted or Stuffed Borders

You can make a white or off-white border extra special by adding stuffed work or another floral motif to the framed section, depending on what best suits your overall quilt design.

Motif balanced around border

Small border print used on both sides of a printed-motif border

Dogteeth and scallops as border-edging patterns

Border styles—2 patchwork borders, 1 printed fabric, 1 stuffed feathers with dogteeth

　　　　Flowers in Appliqué

Amounts of Fabric

The amount of fabric to buy varies for the motifs, ground, and borders. Much depends on the size of the floral motifs, border widths, how many borders you're using, the style of your quilt, and many other variables. However, part of the fun of quilting is collecting fabric. I made *Vintage Rose* (see page 2) and *Rose Wreath* (see page 30) mostly with fabrics I had on hand. I think we all tend to gravitate toward certain colors. So buy fabrics that you really like in those colors and eventually they will find their way into a quilt.

A general rule of thumb when buying fabric for motifs is to buy at least one yard. It is surprising how far you can make that one yard go. However, if you find garlands in your fabric motifs, buy at least 1½ yards (1.4 meters) for medium florals to 3½ yards (3.3 meters) for larger florals. Should you want to use the same fabric in a border-edging design, such as a dogtooth, just add another yard.

The amount of fabric to buy for your borders will vary. My rule of thumb is to pick up "fat quarters" whenever I like a fabric. I buy 1 yard when I *really* like it. And I buy 3 to 6 yards (2.5 to 5.5 meters) when I love it.

The fabric for your ground is the last fabric you will buy in making a motif quilt. You should know which style quilt (medallion, block, or frame) you will be making and for what size bed. You will need between 5 and 8 yards (4.6 to 7.4 meters).

Fabric Preparation

I prefer to work on fabric right from the store. It is crisp and wonderful to use. Quilts made from these fabrics I save for best occasions and I wash them very rarely. I use new fabric only after checking to make sure that the colors will not bleed. To check for bleeding, cut a small piece of your fabric (with all the colors represented in this small piece) and soak it in a small amount of water. Use the same temperature of water that you plan to use when you wash the quilt. Let it soak for a few minutes, then take it out and lay it on a paper towel. Check the water to see if any bleeding has taken place. Then look at the paper towel under and around the small piece of fabric. If no color bleeds out, you are ready to proceed. Dark colors such as navy and burgundy tend to bleed more. If I plan to wash the quilt a lot, I start out with washed fabric. Wash the fabric in the same way you plan to wash the finished quilt.

Marinating the Colors

Lay out all the fabrics that you plan to use in the quilt where you can easily see them together. I spread my fabrics out over a banister, the ironing board, or some other area I walk by frequently. Let the fabrics sit there for a few days. Every time you walk by, check to see if the colors blend, and if not, pull out the ones that are not right. Let fabrics marinate. The longer you allow them to sit together without pulling any colors out, the more positive you'll become that your quilt will work. This is important to all elements of the quilt—the motifs, the ground, and the borders.

When you are sure all the fabrics will work together, line them up as you plan to use them, the center to the outside border. You can lay the fabric for the ground under the motifs. This will give you a second chance to see if all the fabrics will blend.

Technique: Conventional Appliqué Essentials

In Chapter 1 I discussed needle-turning appliqué and how to use fusible web. You can also choose from these two methods when you're sewing conventional appliqué. There are also two other techniques you might use: basting and freezer paper.

Designs for Conventional Appliqué

Your backyard contains a whole garden of ideas for conventional appliqué patterns. Your other ideas can come from almost anywhere: books, painted china, carved furniture, or stencil designs. Keep an eye out for floral patterns that can be extracted for motifs.

You can reduce or enlarge patterns with a photocopier. Just take in your leaf or other desired object and make a copy any size you wish.

Making a Template

Make a plastic template of the design you wish to use, such as a leaf. Place the template over the leaf and draw the pattern. Cut the template out with paper scissors. Do not add seam allowance.

Basting Technique

Place your template on the right side of your fabric. Draw with a pencil around the template. Leave at least $\frac{1}{2}''$ (1.3cm) between appliqué designs to allow for seam allowance for both pieces. Cut around each design, leaving a $\frac{3}{16}''$ (0.5cm) seam allowance. Clip your inside curves almost to the pencil line, as described on page 8.

Fold under the seam allowance and, with a light-colored thread, use a running stitch to baste around the design. Keep folding as you stitch and make the edge as smooth as possible. Handle any clipped corners gently to prevent the fabric from fraying. When you have stitched all around, make one stitch on top of another as a knot. You can also use a washable glue from Roxanne or a glue stick to hold the design temporarily in place.

Freezer-Paper Technique

Using your template, draw some of the leaves on the freezer paper. Freezer paper can be reused several times if necessary. Cut accurately, as this will be the shape of your leaf or design.

Heat your iron to the cotton setting with no steam. Place the fabric that you wish to appliqué right side up on the ironing board. Place your freezer-paper pattern shiny side down on your fabric. You will need to leave $\frac{1}{4}''$ (0.75cm) all around your pattern for seam allowance, or $\frac{1}{2}''$ (1.3cm) between designs. Press the pattern onto the right side of the fabric, holding the iron on top for several seconds. Your pattern will stick to the fabric (the pattern can easily be removed, if you wish). Iron on the remaining leaves or designs, leaving room for a seam allowance for each design. Cut the designs out of the fabric with the $\frac{1}{4}''$ (0.75cm) seam allowance.

Pin the appliqué to the ground with a safety pin or use a washable glue or glue stick to hold the appliqué in place. Clip inside the curves just before you appliqué, as on page 8.

Simple Treasure
Scented Floral Pillow

I enjoy the light scent of potpourri in a room, and I like to change the scent with the seasons. I have one large Chinese bowl near the front door that I fill with potpourri. The scents blow into the room whenever the door is opened. In the spring I make little floral pillows filled with lavender. The floral pillows blend with the painted bowl and keep the little bits from flying about. Once in a while, I slightly pinch the pillow to enhance the fragrance.

Instructions

1. These little pillows are much nicer when lined. We will treat the lining and the floral cotton as one. Place the right sides of the floral cotton together. Put the lining on either side.

2. Using a ¼" (0.75cm) seam on your sewing machine, start stitching 1" (2.5 cm) from the bottom right corner. Backstitch to ½" (1.3cm) from the bottom edge.

3. Pick up the presser foot, slightly turn the pillow, replace the presser foot, and stitch once. Repeat this process four times more to make a slightly rounded corner. This will keep the corners from being sharply pointed.

4. Continue stitching around the pillow, rounding the corners. Stop 1" (2.5cm) from the last corner and backstitch.

5. Cut off the corners and turn the pillow to the flowered side. Use a pin to ease the corners open. Press.

6. Fill the pillow with your favorite potpourri. Do not overfill. Slip-stitch closed.

7. Sew one button in the center of the pillow, then push the needle to the underside and sew on a second button.

8. Using gold thread, blanket-stitch the gold cord around the edge of your pillow or embellish as you like.

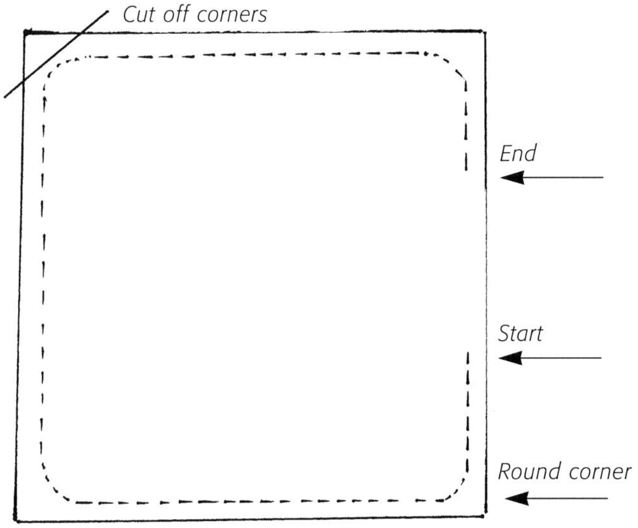

SUPPLIES

2 4½" (11cm) squares floral cotton

2 4½" (11cm) squares cotton for lining

¾ cup (6 oz) potpourri

2 decorative buttons

Gold thread (optional)

½ yard (0.5 meter) gold cord (optional)

Cut off corners

End

Start

Round corner

four

Flower Arranging and Other Techniques

Part of the beauty of having a flower garden is the convenience and fun of cutting flowers to bring into the house. Being able to choose whether to have a whole bouquet of roses or an arrangement of, say, lilies, foxglove, daisies, and peonies, is one of nature's great pleasures. The choices vary with the seasons.

Selecting flowers in a quilt is much the same. Sometimes you will have many choices from your printed floral fabrics, and other times only one motif fabric will do. The challenge is to make the best arrangement no matter what flowers you might have. The results are always satisfying.

You have several techniques to choose from when you create a printed-motif quilt. The technique you opt for depends on your choice of motifs, their size, their shapes, and their colors. You can use a single motif as is; arrange a number of motifs to create a kaleidoscopic pattern or design; make a bouquet contained in a vase, urn, or cornucopia, or tied by a bow; or you can use basic shapes such as circles, ovals, and hearts to form a wreath in which you place individual flowers. These choices are available to you whether you're designing the center of a medallion quilt or a framed quilt. They also work well in each block of a block-motif quilt.

Flowers A-Bloom, 81″ × 81″ (206cm × 206cm)
Designed and hand-stuffed by Judy Severson,
hand-quilted by Toni Fisher

Preparing the Ground

First prepare the fabric that you will be using for the ground. Then decide which style of motif quilt you will be making: medallion, block, or framed. The center medallion might be from 12″ to 42″ (30cm to 107cm), blocks can vary from 10″ to 16″ (25cm to 41cm), and a framed quilt can range from 72″ to 84″ (183cm to 213cm) or more. When I am not sure of the exact size I want, I always make the block a few inches larger; after all, it is easy to cut the block down to a smaller size.

Once you have decided on the size, add ½″ (1.3cm) for your seam allowance and cut out your block. Fold this square in half and iron in the crease. Then fold it in half again in the other direc-

This was inspired by a quilt from the Philadelphia Museum of Art. Photos of the quilt have been published in many quilt books. I always loved the large central basket with four wonderful borders all around it. The center block is 28″ (71cm) square. I filled the basket with flowers from four different fabrics. A garland of tulips surrounds the basket with a scalloped border-edging design. The first border is a loose border stripe design that I also used for some of the flowers in the basket. The second border is a stuffed feather border with two border-edging designs. The inside border-edging design on this second border is a repeat of the curved design from the center medallion. The outside border edging of this second border is created by placing one of the scallops between two of the other scallops. I then repeated that design to make the border edging continuous.

tion and press so you can locate the center of the block. If your block will have several motifs, it is best to iron in diagonal lines through the block as well. Fold the block in half on the diagonal and press, but without losing the first two creases. Then fold it again on the other diagonal and press.

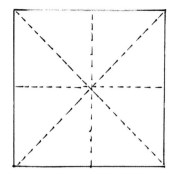

Ground fabric with fold lines for center of square

Once you have the creases in your ground, you are ready to lay the motif or motifs onto the ground fabric. You will need to start thinking about whether your medallion or block will be used on point or square. This decision might influence the way you place the motifs.

Single-Motif Bouquets

Using a single motif as the center of a medallion, block, or framed quilt is one way to start your quilt. Follow the directions in Chapter 2 for selecting and cutting out a motif, whether it is a single flower or group of flowers. Then try placing your motif in the center of the block.

Evening Star (see page vi), a block-style quilt, has a single motif in the center: a group of flowers that looks like a single bouquet tied with a bow. The medallion quilt *Blue Rose* (see page 80) uses a single motif with feathers filling the center block. *Summer Flowers* (see page 94), a block quilt, again has a single flower in the center.

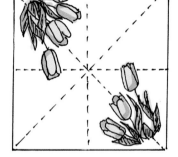

Turning motifs

Kaleidoscope Designing

When I'm trying to decide how to position my motifs on my ground, I like to use a kaleidoscope technique. Slowly turn the two motifs to see how they fit together as you turn them. Continue turning until you've looked at every angle. Add two more motifs so you have four. Place them on your ground and again slowly turn them to see if an interesting center emerges. Add more of the same motifs if you think it necessary. Notice how they seem to fit together.

Combining motifs

Flowers in Appliqué

You might want to select another motif from the same fabric or another fabric with complementary colors. Cut out the motif and again think of the kaleidoscope. Start with one of the original motifs and add two of the second motifs in the corners, as mentioned above. Move the second motifs in a spinning circle, and then move them towards the center while turning them. Try them on the different crease lines and move them from the center and out again while turning them. Next add a second original motif, making two original motifs with the four secondary ones. Keep moving them on the creased lines and spinning them as above. Then try two more of the original and continue to see if there is a pleasing combination.

You can add other motifs to make different patterns in your block. If your block is large, it might accommodate a variety of motifs. Look for a balance when arranging your motifs. Turn the block on all four sides as a final check to see if it is balanced.

Flower Arranging

Another way to work out designs for the center of a block is by arranging the flowers into bouquets. You can tie the bouquets with a bow, place them in a vase or urn, or have them emerge from a cornucopia. Arranging the flower motifs this way, of course, is similar to real-life flower arranging.

Before you start arranging flowers, be they fabric or real, you need to choose a container. You can take designs of bases from quilt books, decorator magazines, floral catalogs, or other publications. You can easily enlarge the designs on a copier, in proportion to the flowers you wish to use and the size of the ground. Next, select a fabric that gives a feeling of that container. For example, if you are choosing a basket, look for a basket weave fabric. For a vase of marble, marble fabric is available in many colors. Select a fabric that evokes the container.

Once you have the container, place it on your ground fabric on the center line. Measure the height of the container. Move the container down from the center line one and a half times the container size to start with. A general rule of thumb is that your container is one-third and the bouquet is two-thirds. This will get you started, but you can easily move the container around at any point before you appliqué.

Making Floral Bouquets

By studying a real floral bouquet, you can learn some lessons to keep in mind when you are arranging floral motifs.

- The flowers that are closest to the container should be very dense, with stems and other flowers in back of them. You should not be able to see any ground.

- The flowers farthest away from the container should be more spread out, to show some of the background around the flowers.

- You should be able to draw an imaginary stem line from the base of the flower into the container, even though the stem is not showing.

- The flowers closest to the container should be larger and stronger in color. Choose flowers that are small in size and lighter in color to be farthest away from the container.

Have at least two, but preferably five or six, different floral-motif fabrics that you use for this arrangement. Cut out several groups of flowers from different parts of the fabric and from other fabrics. Trim the flower or groups of flowers, leaving ¼" (0.75cm) seam allowance as discussed on page 37.

Start with the flowers you will use as a focal point. Arrange them in the center of your block. Place some flowers hanging over the container and some coming up from the container. Once you have one group close to the container, place some flowers where

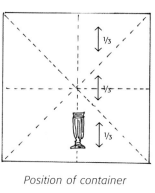

Position of container

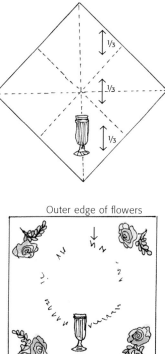

Outer edge of flowers

↑ ¼" seam allowance

Flowers in Appliqué

the outer limits of the bouquet might be. Keep in mind the image of a real floral arrangement. The bouquet does not have to be perfectly round; leave some ground showing. Slowly add other flowers as needed to fill in the bouquet.

Add leaves to the arrangement—a few around the outside edges and one or two peeking from behind the focal point. They help to set off the flowers.

When you think you are finished with the arrangement, turn the block upside down and see if it is still balanced. You might have to add a few more leaves or small flowers in some places. Many times when we think of balance we look right and left. Remember to look on the diagonal as well.

Creating Shapes

You can use basic shapes such as circles (wreaths), hearts, ovals, and other outlines to make a motif quilt. Decide on a shape and draw it to scale on your ground with a light pencil mark. This type of design is best suited to individual flowers with leaves or single-leaf and single-flower motifs.

You can work with either fabric motifs or paper cutouts when you begin your design. Once you decide on the technique you will use, work with the actual fabric motifs.

Remember that flowers have a direction. The flower petals face up or out, and the stems go down and are hidden under other flowers to create the shape you desire.

You can achieve a formal arrangement of the shapes through precise placement of each flower and leaf. A more informal arrangement will result from a looser and less precise placement of many different flowers. Whatever arrangement you choose, you are creating a unique design, a quilt of your own.

Basic shapes for blocks

Other Inspirations for Center Medallions or Blocks

One piece of fabric, like a toile, a floral fabric, or a whole printed basket fabric, can make a perfect center to a medallion or can be combined with other floral motifs in an alternating-block design. Perhaps you can cut some of the motifs in the blocks from the fabric you will use in one of the borders.

Besides using motifs for the center of your medallion or for blocks, you might choose a simple patchwork star or other patchwork design. The reason for choosing an uncomplicated patchwork design is to let the beauty of the printed motifs stand out.

Octagon Essentials

You can use an octagon shape either as the center of a medallion, as in *English Garden* on page 77 or as a block. An easy way to cut an octagon shape is to fold a square, of any size you wish, into eighths. Measuring from the center, fold the width you desire, and cut off the corners at a right angle. This shape is difficult to sew because it involves four additional corners; proceed with caution.

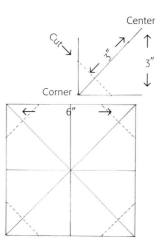

Making an octagon

Chintz Block, *mid-nineteenth century, Shelburne Museum, Shelburne Vermont.*
Photograph by Ken Burris

Flowers in Appliqué

Technique: Appliquéing a Flower Arrangement

Once you have your flower arrangement laid out on your block, you need to prepare it for appliquéing.

Making a Pattern

I find it best to make a pattern to preserve the original design. Using tracing paper, draw around the outside edge of each flower. Note the color or any identifying parts on the pattern to make certain which flower or leaf goes where.

Marking the Ground

With a pencil, lightly mark the ground where the outside edges of leaves and flowers lie. Mark the bottom and sides of the container in a few places on the ground; if it shifts you will be able to put it back in place.

Glueing and Trimming

Working from the outside in, use a washable glue from Roxanne or washable glue stick to temporarily glue the flowers and leaves in place if you are going to sew. If you are using the fusible web, also start from the outside in. Trim away excess fabric that goes behind the other flowers as you go. You want to have the least number of fabric layers possible. This is true whether you use the fusible web or a needle and thread.

As you approach the center you do not want to have the ground showing. In a real arrangement other leaves and flowers would be behind the flowers in the center. Place a small piece of a leaf between the flowers if the ground fabric is showing.

Appliquéing the Flowers

Once the flower arrangement is stabilized with fusible web or washable glue stick, it is ready for you to sew. Use a satin stitch on the machine or a blanket stitch by hand for a more decorative stitch. The least obtrusive method for appliqué, as described in Chapter 1, is the slip stitch sewn by hand. This stitch also shows off the beauty of the motifs to their best advantage.

Simple Treasure
Floral Eyeglass Case

After years of tossing my eyeglasses into my purse at the last minute, I decided that if I had more than one eyeglass case, it would be easier to take better care of them. It seemed only natural to pull out some florals from my quilt fabric collection and make several cases for my eyewear. Using a large floral fabric for the outside and a contrasting fabric on the inside, I found it easy to make several cases at the same time. This project was a great way to use bits of fabric that I loved but that I had thought I would never be able to find a use for again.

Instructions

8" (20cm) square floral fabric
for outside

8" (20cm) square cotton batt

8" (20cm) square inner-lining
fabric

8" (20cm) square contrasting
lining fabric

Silver marking pencil

1. Draw the eyeglass case pattern onto your floral fabric with the silver pencil. Cut the pattern out of the floral fabric.

2. Working on the right side of the floral fabric, mark your quilting pattern with the silver pencil as follows: Draw a diagonal line through the center of the fabric from corner to corner. The line should be at a 45° angle. Then draw a 1½" (4cm) grid all over the floral fabric, starting at the line you've drawn.

3. Using the pattern and your silver pencil, mark and cut out your inner lining and cotton batt.

4. Lay your cotton batt on top of the inner lining, and then lay the floral fabric on the batt. Pin around the edges to hold the layers together. Set your sewing machine at about 12 stitches per inch (5 stitches per cm). Sew along the gridlines you marked on your fabric, starting with the middle line and working out in one direction. Turn the fabric. Again start stitching in the middle and work your way out.

5. Lay your quilted floral fabric right sides together with the lining. Place a ruler straight across the top of the case and measure down 1½" (4cm). Place a mark at that point on the two outside edges on the seam allowance. See pattern.

6. Starting at the first mark and ¼" (0.75 cm) in from the edge, sew across the top of the case to the other mark. Trim the seam to ⅛" (0.4cm) at the two curves and turn right sides out. Use the eraser end of a pencil to help make the case even and smooth. Press the case, checking to make sure the lining is inside. Topstitch the same top edge in ¼" (0.75cm).

7. Fold your case in half, right sides together, and pin the two sides and bottom together. Starting just above where the mark is on the sides, stitch around to the bottom, making a backstitch at the top and bottom.

8. Trim the bottom corners with scissors and turn the right sides out. Use the eraser end of a pencil to help square up the two corners.

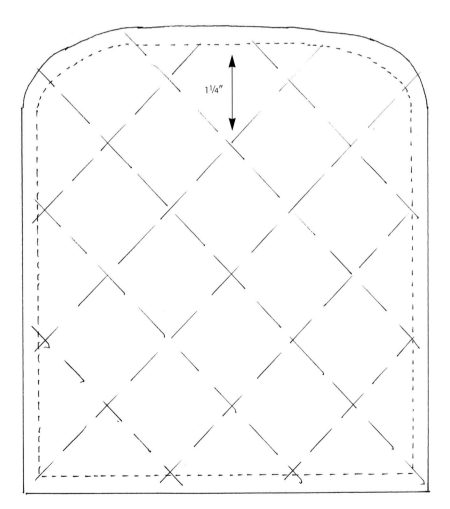

1¼"

Eyeglass case with quilting lines

five

Borders and Beyond

he center block or medallion is the focal point of your printed-motif quilt, but the borders frame your center and add to the overall look of the quilt. The borders should not take a backseat to the center; in fact, they may give the quilt its character as in my *Angel Quilt* (see page 56).

One way of creating a harmonious quilt is to repeat a floral fabric in the border that you have already used in the medallion or in one of the blocks. It's also a good idea to have the borders be a little larger or darker in color as you move outward from the center to give the quilt balance.

Number of Borders

After you've designed the center of your quilt, decide how many borders you will add. If you are making a bed quilt (versus a wall hanging), you can lay the medallion on the bed. Measure the distance from the medallion to the edge or break of the bed. This area could be the size of your first border to surround the medallion. The next border might extend from the edge of the bed down to the top ruffle of the skirt — 12″ to 16″ (30cm to 41cm). This will be your outside border if you are using a dust ruffle.

Angel Quilt, 83" × 83" (211cm × 211cm)
Designed and hand-stuffed by Judy Severson,
machine-quilted by Shirley Greenhoe

If you want the quilt to extend to the floor, you might create another border about 14" (35.5cm) wide, the usual drop of a bed skirt. This size will vary depending on the bed you are using. Once you decide on the size of your outermost border, you can plan additional borders to fit between your medallion and your outside border. There are no hard and fast rules on the width of borders. Have a general plan in mind but be flexible. You might think of better ideas as you are working.

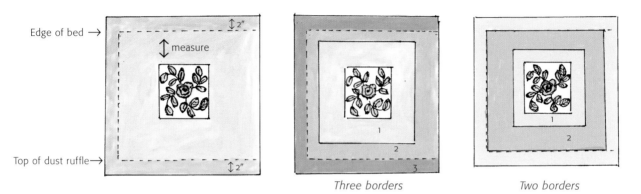

Three borders   Two borders

I started this quilt in a class that was based on making a much smaller quilt. *We* made the patchwork star on point with one inner border. *Then* we added the triangles and a dark border to complete the quilt. But those four wonderful white triangles seemed to call out for printed motifs. *So I* chose four different groups of flowers to appliqué in the corners. *After* finishing that appliqué, *I* felt the quilt needed yet more borders. *So I* added another border using the method of making vines described in this chapter. *I* then added three more borders. *The* first uses a repeat of the dark border; the second repeats the patchwork *I* used in the center; and the outermost border is a solid piece of fabric in the same colors. *I* used only one yard (0.9 meter) of fabric for the motifs as well as some of the leaves and flowers from the black border fabric.

Square or Rectangular Quilts

Some quilters prefer to make rectangular quilts rather than square quilts. Rectangular quilts allow extra length for the pillows under the quilt. Other quilters put their pillows on top, and so prefer to make square quilts. Another advantage of square quilts is that you can rotate them to keep them from fading. Also, in the morning when you are placing the quilt back on the bed, it will not make any difference which end is up. (However, if your medallion center is a floral basket, rotation is not practical on a wall or bed!)

In Chapter 3 I briefly discussed the different types of borders: motif, floral fabric, appliqué, patchwork, and quilted or stuffed borders. Now let's look more closely at each.

Motif Borders

The shapes of the motifs will help you determine how to use them. If the motifs are upright and tightly grouped flowers, they can be spaced evenly around the border. If the motifs are different sizes, the flower groups must be balanced around the border.

Some motifs seem to flow out from other flowers and form a ready-made border. You can arrange them to go around the border in one continuous direction. Or you might make the motifs come out of the corner and meet in the middle. They can also come out of the middle and meet at the corner. Use any combination that works with the flowers.

Garlands that you find in the repeat of floral fabrics (discussed in Chapter 3) are wonderful ready-made borders. When you come to a corner, you can either add a few other flowers or cut out a few flowers to make the garland turn the corner.

Floral Fabric Borders

Floral fabrics are traditionally used as the outermost border in motif quilts. The flowers do not need to be large. These borders are usually about 8″ to 16″ (20cm to 41cm) wide. The color or colors should complement the rest of the quilt.

Upright motifs equally spaced

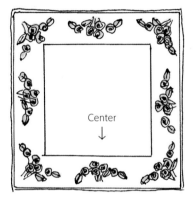

Grouped motifs

Continuous motifs in inner border. In outer border they are arranged in center and corners.

The motif was cut in half and a leaf was added.

↓ Motif ↓

Rounding a corner with whole motif

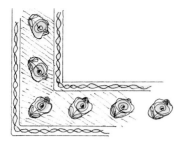

Combining small border fabric with other floral fabrics

Dogteeth

Curved

Other

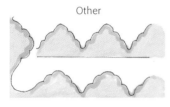

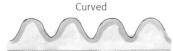

Border-edging designs—size has been reduced

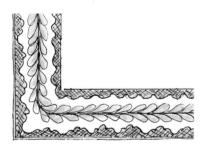

Border-edging designs used with feathers

Border-edging using stair steps

You can also use a border print, which is fabric designed specifically for use as a border. Border prints are readily available now at most quilt stores and are becoming increasingly popular. The larger border prints can be used as is, but many of the border prints tend to be small—1″ to 2″ (2.5cm to 5cm) wide. Border prints can be used alone on the outside edge of the quilt or you can combine a narrow border with another wider piece of fabric to form a larger border.

Border-Edging Essentials

You can create border-edging designs, such as dogteeth and curved borders, using strips of fabric. The finished border edgings are usually 2″ to 3″ (5cm to 7.5cm) tall. You can add these designs to one or both sides of a border.

You might also add motifs or other appliqué to these borders. Quilting or stuffed feathers are a nice addition with border edging. The edging helps to frame the border and give it strength. Stair steps, another type of border edging, can be made to any height. Stair steps are usually on the outer edge of a border, either used alone or with one or two steps on the inner edge of a border.

Adding Border Edging

You can add border edging to the outside of a border by cutting a strip of fabric the length of your outside border. The strip can be any width, but 2″ (5cm) finished is average. For a 2″ border edging, cut the strip 2½″ (6.3cm) wide to include seam allowance on both sides. Using a ¼″ (0.75cm) seam allowance and basting stitch—8 stitches to the inch (3 stitches to the centimeter)—on the machine, sew the strip to the border. Start stitching ½″ (1.3cm) in from the edge and stop ¼″ (0.75cm) from the end of the border strip. You can sew all four sides of the border strip or add one at a time.

To make mitered corners, draw a light pencil line on the border edging at a 45° angle, starting at the corner. Trim the outside edge ¼″ (0.75cm) from the miter. Press the edge under using the pencil line for your guide. The border edging under the miter can also be trimmed in the same way. The border edging can then lie under the mitered corner. Attach it with a safety pin until you're ready to appliqué.

Measuring for Dogteeth

Dogteeth can vary in length, but generally they are 2″ (5cm) wide. To make dogteeth, measure the length of your border without seam allowance. If that measurement does not divide evenly by two, vary the size of the dogtooth so that it is easily divisible into the length measurement. If you are using 2″ (5cm) for the width of your dogteeth, measure in 2″ (5cm) from what will be your finished border. Place a light pencil mark ½″ (0.3cm) in from the edge. Place the next mark 1″ (2.5cm) over but at the top, ¼″ (0.75cm) in from the edge. Continue marking every inch, alternating top and bottom, around the quilt.

When you are ready to appliqué, cut down almost to the lower mark that will be the bottom of the dogtooth. Trim away the border strip to about ³⁄₁₆″ (0.5cm). Fold the edge under so you have a straight line from your two points. Appliqué as suggested in Chapter 3. Cut a few dogteeth at a time as you work around the quilt.

Curved Border-Edging Designs

Curved border-edging designs can be adjusted to fit any length border. Decide on the style of edging you will use. The highest part, or the center of the border-edging design, is called the hill. The lowest part, the area between the hills, is called the valley. You can create corners by joining the units at the hill or in the valley. It is easiest to join at the valley because then the corner is adjustable.

Freezer Paper for Edging Designs

Cut a plastic template for one unit of your border-edging design. First measure the length of your unit from valley to valley and divide into the finished length of your border so you will know how many units to cut. Cut a freezer-paper pattern the length of your border. You can fold the paper in half so you will be cutting two

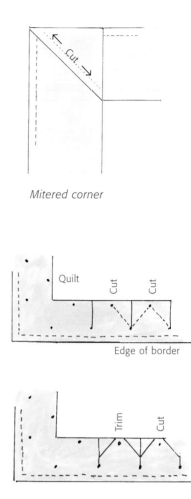

Mitered corner

Measuring for dogteeth

Flowers in Appliqué

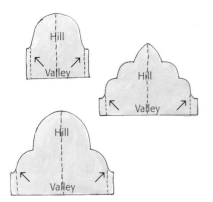

Border unit designs

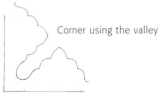

Corner using the valley

←Length of corner→

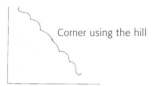

Corner using the hill

←Length of corner→

Corner-edging choices

Adjusting border edging

units at a time. Use paper clips to hold the paper together if necessary. You will reuse the pattern on each side as you go around the quilt.

Lay out the freezer-paper pattern on the border so you can see in advance how the corner will work out. Decide whether you prefer the pattern to meet at the hill or in the valley. Make the necessary adjustment of the corner if you are joining at the valley. Cut a freezer-paper pattern of the corner.

You can iron the freezer-paper pattern onto the border edge. Use the cotton setting on your iron with no steam. Start in the middle of the border. Find the center of your freezer paper by folding it in half, or count the units you will be using on half the border. Lay the shiny side of the paper down along the edge of your border, and press by leaving the iron in place several seconds and working toward the corner. Freezer paper will stick to itself when ironed, so slightly overlay the edging pattern when you need two pieces together. Press the corner pattern in place. Trim to 3/16″ (0.5cm) as you go along the border-edging strip. Then appliqué as shown in Chapter 3.

Appliqué Borders

You can add other conventional appliqué patterns to the printed motifs in a border, or—as with most of the quilts in this book—you can use the motifs by themselves. Use individual appliqué patterns of flowers much the same way as motifs. The appliqué patterns are easier to use, since they can be reversed. Simply turn the patterns over on the fabric to make leaves or flowers go in the opposite direction. Motifs, on the other hand, are printed in only one direction.

I think that the best appliqué border you can make is a vine that carries your eye around the border. You can use either plain or printed calico fabric. You can add any leaves or flowers to your vine. Your garden contains a ready supply of patterns. Later in this chapter I will show you an easy technique to make vines fit any borders.

Patchwork Borders

Simple patchwork borders are often the best choice in motif quilts. You want the motifs to catch the eye, and patchwork gives you greater flexibility to add colors that will enhance the whole quilt. The smaller the patchwork design, the smaller the floral pattern can be. When you use larger-floral fabrics, use the larger patchwork designs to show off the fabric.

Some of the patchwork designs that are often used in motif quilts are squares of all sizes and patterns using triangular shapes. The patterns bear such names as *Four-patch, Nine-patch, Sawtooth, Windmills, Streak of Lightning, Lost Ships, Delectable Mountains, Broken Dishes,* and *Diamonds.* Stars that you often see in borders include the *Eight-Pointed Star* and *Evening Star.*

Pumpkinseed is a patchwork pattern that you can use in a single row or in multiple rows to form a border. Since it is a little tricky to do it as patchwork, you can appliqué pumpkinseed instead. See *Blue Rose* on page 80.

Patchwork is a good way to carry out or emphasize the colors in your motifs. Remember that you have endless choices of fabric to make your quilt unique.

Quilted and Stuffed Borders

I love to use feather designs either alone or combined with border-edging designs in motif quilts. There are so many feather designs that I discuss them at length in Chapter 9.

I also love to use beautiful leaf and flower designs, which I quilt and stuff in my borders. You can combine the leaves and flowers with flower motifs, as well as with patchwork patterns such as *Delectable Mountains* and *Evening Star.*

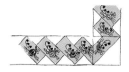

Nine-patch border—small floral fabric

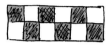

Brick border—medium floral fabric

Four-patch

Blocks

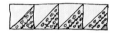

Nine-patch

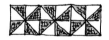

Sawtooth

Windmills

Streak of Lightning

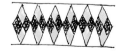

Diamonds

Pumpkinseed

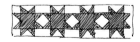

Evening Star

Delectable Mountains

Eight-Pointed Star

Lost Ships

Flowers in Appliqué

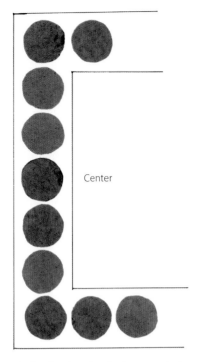

Single-vine border: laying out circles

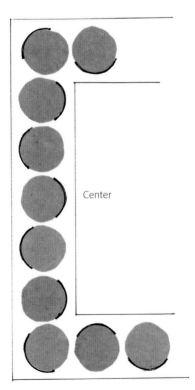

Single-vine border: marking circles

Technique: Designing Vines for Appliqué Borders

This technique was inspired by an innovative teacher, Lucy Hilty, who used it to teach a class on drafting feathers. It works equally well as an easy way to design continuous vines around your border.

First decide on the design of your corners and the number of vines you want to undulate around the border. You can design your vine directly on the border fabric although I think it's easier to work on dressmaking paper, which is available at quilt stores. The first few times you design vine borders, you may want to see the entire border, so buy enough paper to cover the length of the border completely. There is a 1″ (2.5cm) grid on the paper so it is easy to draw out the length and width of your border. Be sure to include the corner in your border design.

Single-Vine Border

The basic vine border is a single vine that undulates around the border. Measure the width and length of your border. Using the grid paper, draw the border and include both corners. Mark the center of the border with a line.

With a compass, draw a circle on a plain piece of paper. The circle should be ½″ to 1″ (1.3cm to 2.5cm) smaller than the width of the border. Cut out eight more circles that are the same size as the first circle. Lay the circles across the border. Start by placing one in each corner and one in the middle. Then fill in the border with as many circles as necessary. Space them evenly across. You will always need an odd number of circles to make the vine turn the corner.

Marking the Vine

Starting at the outside edge of the corner, use a pencil to mark the bottom half of the first circle. Then mark just the top half of the next circle. Continue alternating, marking the circles until you reach the other corner. Remove the circles from the paper. Join the lines you have drawn together with a slight **S** curve.

You can create a more gentle curve by removing two circles from the border. Leave the circles in the center and the corner. Adjust the remaining circles so they are evenly spaced.

Single-Vine Corners

With a single-vine border you can make four different basic corners just by adjusting the circles. The four corners are the **C** curve, the horseshoe, the loop, and the inverted loop. Other loops can be made along your border depending on its length.

Leaving Room for More Leaves

When you use a circle this size for your template, you can add leaves and motifs only on the inside of the curves. There is not enough room for them on the outside curve. If you wish to add leaves on both sides of the vine, use circles that are just half as large as the border. Cut out about 11 smaller circles and place them evenly across the border as previously discussed, this time leaving more space between each circle.

Draw your vine, starting at the outside edge of the circle at the corner. Now there is room for leaves on both sides of the vine. You can adjust the circles to be closer at the center or in the corners for a different look. Have fun experimenting.

Double-Vine Border

The double vine is created basically the same way as the single vine. Determine the size of your circles by choosing whether to have leaves on one side or both sides of your vine. Lay out your circles on the border. This time, however, mark the top and bottom of each circle. Starting at the corner, connect the circles with a gentle **s** curve in the same manner as a single vine.

When adding the second vine on that border, start at the outside of the second circle from the corner. Cross the first vine to the inside of the next circle and continue to the outside of the next circle. Continue across to the second circle from the corner.

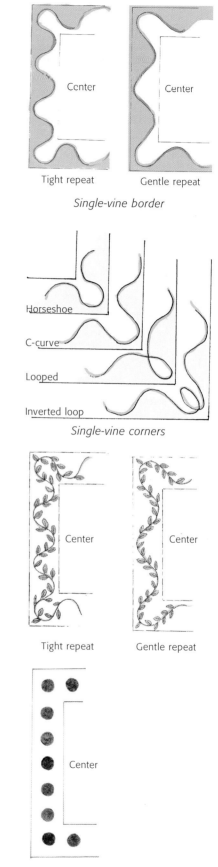

Tight repeat   Gentle repeat

Single-vine border

Horseshoe
C-curve
Looped
Inverted loop

Single-vine corners

Center   Center

Tight repeat   Gentle repeat

Center

Circles laid out for vine with leaves on both sides

Flowers in Appliqué

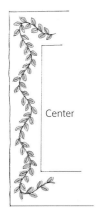

Adding leaves on both sides of vine

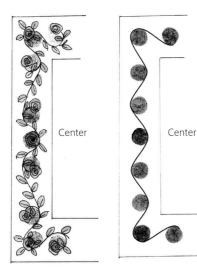

Arranging circles to vary the vine

Double vine using circles half the width of the border

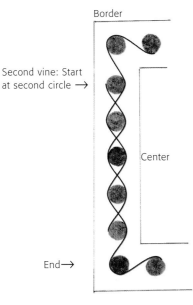

Border

Second vine: Start at second circle →

Center

End→

Adding second vine

Double-Vine Corners

There are two basic corners you can use with double vines: the cable and the knot.

The cable corner starts out like the single-vine corner, with the vine passing from the inside circle to the outside of the corner circle. The second vine will pull across the corner circle gently.

You can easily make the knot border by placing two circles in the corner instead of one. Adjust all other circles so they are evenly spaced. Again, start at the single-vine border at the circle next to the double-circle corner. Draw a line from the inside out around both circles in the corner. Continue the line to the next single circle on the inside.

Adding Stems, Leaves, and Flowers

There are endless possibilities when you add stems, leaves, and flowers to your vine border. The choice is yours. You can create more formal arrangements by placing leaves and flowers on either side of the stem and making each unit identical. For a less formal vine, vary a few leaves or flowers but leave some units the same to create a balanced effect. Place some flowers or leaves right on the vine to make it more realistic.

Leaves from your garden or a friend's garden make wonderful patterns and will make the quilt more personal. See Chapter 3 for suggestions on using patterns in appliqué. You can use leaves that are all the same size or try many variations until you find the most pleasing vine.

When you have completed your design, you are ready to transfer the design to your border. With continuous vines, it is easiest to sew the border onto the quilt before you appliqué. In Chapter 6 I will show you how to add a border to keep the quilt square.

Transferring the Design

Transfer the pattern by making templates or using a light box. If you are using templates, you will need to make one for the corner and one for a side unit. Start with template plastic that is the same size as the unit. Place the plastic over your pattern and draw the vine, leaves, and stems. Before you cut it out, check to see if all the units are the same. There might be slight variations, so adjust to the average. Cut the template along the vine.

Place the whole corner unit in the corner of your border to check the placement of the vine. Remove half the corner unit to obtain the stem line. Lightly mark the fabric with a pencil. You can mark where the stems, vines, flowers, and leaves intersect the vine. Remove that half of the template and place the other half to mark where the stems and leaves on the other side will go. If you are not sure which mark is for which side, a small arrow at the stem will remind you.

Place half the side unit up against the corner unit, and again mark as above. Proceed around the border, using the different units until the border is completely marked.

Bias Strips for the Vine

You will need to cut bias strips of fabric to create your vine. The amount of fabric will vary with the length of your vine and the bias strips you use. One-half yard of fabric will make 12 yards (11 meters) of 1¼″ (3.2cm) strips. Strips are cut from the fabric at a

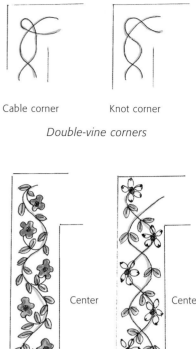

Cable corner   Knot corner

Double-vine corners

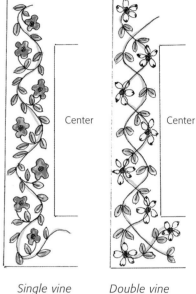

Single vine   Double vine

Formal vines

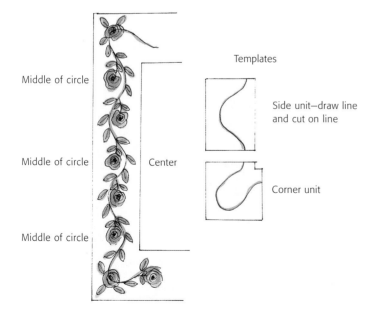

Middle of circle

Middle of circle

Middle of circle

Center

Templates

Side unit—draw line and cut on line

Corner unit

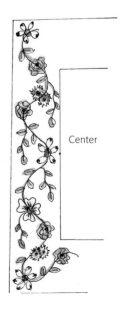

Center

Informal vine

Flowers in Appliqué

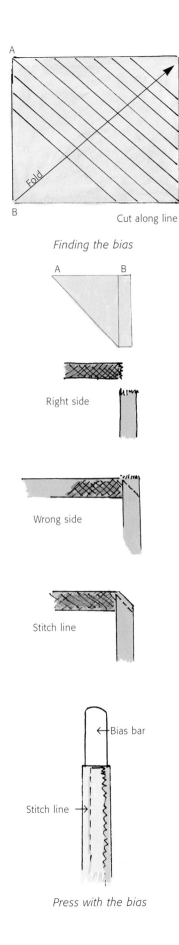

Finding the bias

Right side

Wrong side

Stitch line

← Bias bar

Stitch line →

Press with the bias

45° angle. Fold the corner of the fabric to find the bias. Press the fabric and cut along the press line. Cut out 1¼″ (3.2cm) strips.

Sew strips right sides together by laying the strips perpendicular to each other. Stitch on the diagonal and trim the seams to ¼″ (0.75cm). Always press the seam in one direction.

Using Bias Bars

I like to use bias bars to make the vine an even size. Bias bars are 12″ (30cm) metal bars of varying widths that you can purchase from a quilt store. I like to use the ¼″ (0.75cm) wide bar.

Once the bias strip is continuous and the seams are all pressed in the same direction, fold the bias strip in half. Stitch ¼″ (0.75cm) from the fold. I like to put the bias bar in the fold, letting the strip run through my fingers until the end of the bias bar. Move the bias bar back down through the unstitched bias along the fold, and stitch in ¼″ (0.75cm). You have to be careful not to let the bias bar go under the needle, but this method allows for an even strip. Trim the seam allowance to ¼″ (0.75cm).

Once you've stitched the vine, place the bias bar back in the vine. Adjust the seam and seam allowance to one side of the bar, and press. This way the seam and seam allowance will be on the back side and will not show. Press the rest of the vine in the same way.

Basting Vine to Border

Now you are ready to baste the vine onto your border. With a single vine, start basting the bias strip on your penciled stem line somewhere between the corner and the middle of the border. Your eyes tend to focus more closely at these areas. If you have a flower or leaf that will cover the joining of the beginning or end of the stem, start there. Use a running stitch all around.

You can now baste your leaves and flowers in place, or you can glue them on with a washable glue stick. You can also use printed motifs as the flowers and leaves, either on a vine by themselves or combined with other conventionally appliquéd leaves and stems. See *Angel Quilt* on page 56.

Bordered Pincushion

$\mathcal{I}$ wanted to create a pincushion that would show off
some of my special hat pins. *It* needed to be large enough
to hold the long pins, but *I* also wanted it to be special in
its own right. *S*tarting with a medium-size floral fabric
for the center, *I* accented it with $1/4"$ (0.75cm) of bright
colored fabric, then framed it in a darker calico.
I added beads and embroidery stitches to complete the
pincushion.

Instructions

1. Select a flower or group of flowers from your medium-floral fabric. Cut a 3″ (7.5cm) square around the flowers.

2. Cut a ¾″ (2cm) strip of contrasting fabric about 19″ (48cm) long. Cut two 3″ (7.5cm) long pieces from the strip and stitch them to the opposite sides of the square, using a ¼″ (0.75cm) seam allowance.

3. Cut a strip of calico border that is 2″ (5cm) wide and 19″ (48cm) long. Cut two 3″ (7.5cm) long pieces from the calico strip and stitch them to the contrasting strips.

4. Cut two 6½″ (16.5cm) long pieces from the contrasting strip and sew them to the top and bottom of the pincushion.

5. Cut two 6½″ (16.5cm) long pieces of calico border strip and add them to the top and bottom.

6. Embellish the top as desired with stitches and beads.

7. Cut three 6½″ (16.5cm) squares of calico border fabric for the back and inner lining (a lining will make the pincushion feel more substantial). Scraps of other fabrics may be substituted for the lining.

8. Place right sides of your pincushion together. Then place the lining fabric on either side of the top and bottom. Starting from the center of one side, stitch ¼″ (0.75cm) in all around the pincushion, leaving a 1½″ (4cm) opening. Round the corners as shown on page 39 for the Scented Floral Pillow.

9. Turn right sides out, using your fingers or the eraser end of a pencil to open all the seams. Fill with stuffing and then close the seam with a slip stitch. You can then add embroidery or a trim to the edge.

1 3″ (7.5cm) square of medium-floral fabric

1 ¾″ × 19″ (2cm × 48cm) strip of contrasting fabric

¼ yard (0.25 meter) of calico for border

Stuffing

Trim for outside edge

Embroidery thread, beads, and small braid for outside edge (optional)

Chintz Medallion,
108¾" × 113⅛" (276cm × 287cm)
Mrs. James Lusby, Washington, D.C., 1837–1838
National Museum of American History,
Smithsonian Institution

A Gallery of Antique and Contemporary Quilts

I've been studying quilts since 1979, and chintz quilts have always caught my eye. With their exquisite floral fabrics and their fresh-looking designs, no two are alike, even though they are made with some of the same fabrics. They have an elegance that is hard to find in other styles of quilts.

It has always amazed me how many of these quilts have survived over time. I think the fortunate families who inherit the chintz quilts must be especially touched by their beauty and so take care to safeguard them.

Although I'm not a historian, I don't think a person can get involved in quilt making without becoming curious about the origins of these quilts. The following pages will help you understand the influences that led me to printed-motif quilts. For more extensive reading in this area, I recommend the fine works of Barbara Brackman, Dorothy Osler, and others listed in Books for Inspiration (see page 149).

Chintz Quilts

The first motif-appliqué quilts apparently were fashioned in direct response to the unavailability of cotton chintz fabrics during the eighteenth century. Such fabrics had been exported from India to Europe during the sixteenth and seventeenth centuries. The original imports were *Palampores*, fabrics featuring printed medallions and usually based on the tree-of-life motif. These fabrics were made into whole-cloth quilts or bedcovers. The fabrics were finely made and printed and they became extremely popular. However, their popularity—for quilted bedcovers, articles of clothing, and home furnishings—alarmed the English silk and woolen-goods manufacturers of the time. To protect their competitive interests, these manufacturers caused the English Parliament to ban both the importation of cotton cloth and the decorative printing of such cloth. In response to this shortage, seamstresses stretched their available chintzes by cutting from them the designs of flowers, urns, birds, or trees, and applying these cuttings to a ground cloth to form an appliqué. Although the first motif quilts were probably made in England, they were certainly made by the American colonists early in the eighteenth century and soon came to be thought of as an American craft.

A major influence in early American quilt making was an Englishman and fabric printer by the name of John Hewson, who at the beckoning of Benjamin Franklin immigrated to this country just before the Revolutionary War. Hewson brought with him the skills of cotton fabric printing, and produced some fabrics expressly for quilters. A Hewson bedcover or center medallion today is highly prized; it is considered representative of the finest of American textile printing of the eighteenth century. Several fine examples of Hewson's work are in the quilt collections of the Winterthur Museum in Delaware and the Cincinnati Art Museum in Ohio.

The motif-appliqué quilt became an American favorite during the Revolutionary War, particularly along the Eastern seaboard. Although the heyday of American motif-appliqué quilts is generally considered to have peaked by 1840, their popularity continued until the war between the states in the mid-nineteenth century. At that

Flowers in Appliqué

Chintz Medallion,
112½″ × 111″ (286cm × 282cm)
American, c. 1830–1850
National Museum of American History,
Smithsonian Institution

A Gallery of Antique and Contemporary Quilts

time the block patterns of the friendship quilts and the colorful and elaborate Baltimore album quilts replaced the central medallion as the predominant quilt motif.

Broderie Perse Quilts

By the end of the nineteenth century, the French term *broderie perse* became fashionable for the motif-appliqué style. *Broderie perse* translates as "Persian embroidery" and refers to a style of elaborate stitching. This type of embroidery was sometimes used to detail certain elements of a design, such as flower stems and stamens, edging around each petal, and other selected motifs, reflecting the emphasis on fine needlework found during the Victorian era.

Motif Quilts Today

In the 1980s several publications encouraged the creation of these motif appliqués. But the only chintz available at that time was from home-decorating stores. It was stiff and difficult to quilt, which discouraged many quilters from using it. Today, however, there are a number of fine cottons with large patterns available that work very well for this purpose, and it appears that a renaissance of the printed-motif quilt is at hand.

Exploring Motif Quilts

Look at each of the floral-motif quilts on these pages. First decide the style of the quilt—medallion, block, or framed. Where is the motif used, in a block or in a border? Can you tell if it is a group of flowers or a flower-on-flower arrangement? Notice if there is other appliqué, patchwork, whole-fabric borders, stuffed work, or embellishing stitches. Now look again at the quilts in the rest of the book to see the versatility of the motif quilt.

Flowers in Appliqué

A Gallery of Antique and Contemporary Quilts

Chintz Block,

109″ × 112″ (277cm × 284cm)

Virginia, Mid-nineteenth century

Shelburne Museum. Photograph by Ken Burris

Chintz Medallion,

84½″ × 104″ (215cm × 264cm)

American, Before 1850

Winterthur Museum

Chintz Framed, 115¼″ × 124″ (293cm × 315cm)

Achsah Goodwin Wilkins, Baltimore, c. 1820–1840

National Museum of American History,

Smithsonian Institution

Chintz Star of Bethlehem,

106″ × 106″ (269cm × 269cm)

American, Early nineteenth century

Shelburne Museum. Photograph by Ken Burris

Flowers in Appliqué

Vintage Blossoms,
63″ × 63″ (160cm × 160cm)
Jeri Thomason,
Corte Madera, CA, 1997

Broderie Perse Medallion,
88″ × 88″ (223.5cm × 223.5cm)
Martha Noha,
Petaluma, CA, 1997

Village Square,
78″ × 78″ (198cm × 198cm)
Bobbi Finley,
San Jose, CA, 1997

English Garden,
86″ × 86″ (218cm × 218cm)
Judy Severson,
Belvedere, CA, 1997

A Gallery of Antique and Contemporary Quilts

six

Creating a Floral Medallion Quilt

A medallion quilt, with its central block and borders, allows you almost unlimited design choices. You can plan a medallion quilt down to the last quilt stitch, or you can be loose and let the quilt grow until it is a finished size. It is always a good idea to plan ahead a little, but be flexible in case you find that very special fabric that will make one last perfect border.

A medallion quilt can be square or rectangular in shape, but it starts with your center block. Let the center be something you love, whether it is a single flower, a special toile, or a bright patchwork star. If you want to create a romantic center block with printed motifs, look at Chapter 4 for ideas.

Whatever you choose to put in the center, plan to fill the whole center. Too much unplanned space will leave the center looking empty. The center is the picture that you will be framing with your borders. Each border should continue to enhance the whole until the quilt is completed.

Blue Rose, 78″ × 78″ (198cm × 198cm)
Designed and hand-stuffed by Judy Severson,
hand-quilted by Toni Fisher

Square or On Point

Square

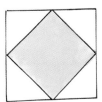

On point

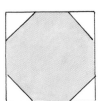

Octagon

Whatever your choice for your center block, it can be arranged in a square or on point. Actually, you can also create a octagon, as shown in Chapter 5.

If you place your center on point, you will create four triangles in the corners that surround the center. These can be a wonderful addition or not, depending on your center and the fabrics you have chosen. Personally, I think the triangles are a great place to add printed motifs.

Figuring the Size of Your Triangles

The size of your triangles is easy to figure. The key is to realize that the triangles are one-quarter the size of the finished center square if you divide the square diagonally from corner to corner. Just remember that you will need to add ¼″ (0.75cm) all around each triangle for your seam allowances.

The triangles will have two equal sides and one longer side. To calculate the size of your triangles, measure all four sides of your center block to make sure it is truly square. If all the sides are the same size, subtract ½″ (1.3cm) from the side measurement (for your seam allowances). The resulting figure is also the measurement for the long side of your corner triangles. For instance, if each of your four sides is 10½″ (26.5cm) long, subtract ½″ from 10½″ (1.3cm from 26.5cm). The answer, 10″ (25cm), is the measurement for the long side of your corner triangles.

I have always loved blue and white china. When I found this blue and white fabric, it reminded me of a Spode plate I had recently seen. Inspired by the china, I used the pumpkinseed patchwork pattern in my quilt and added the small scallops that I loved in the plate design. The floral garlands were already in the rose fabric. I let the other fabrics speak for themselves as borders.

If your block is not square, average the measurements of the four sides. For instance, if one side is 10⅝" (27cm), a second side is 10⅜" (26.4cm), and the remaining two sides are each 10½" (26.5cm), use the average of 10½" (26.5cm) as your measurement. Then subtract ½" (1.3cm) for seam allowances, making the long side of your triangle 10" (25cm).

Now you can create a template for your triangle. First draw a line 10" (25cm) long on scratch paper. Divide that line in half. Starting at the halfway point, draw another line at right angles to the first line, but only half its length, in this case 5" (12.5cm). The top of your second line will become the point of your triangle. Next, draw in the two sides of your triangle. Extend a line from the point of your triangle back down to each end point of your base line. Add a ¼" (0.75cm) seam allowance all around the triangle. You can cut the triangle out of your paper or transfer your drawing to template plastic. When you are ready to mark your fabric for cutting, be sure to lay your triangle on the fabric with the two equal sides of the triangle on the straight of the grain.

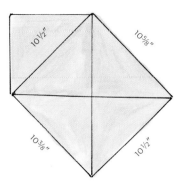

Measuring for the triangle

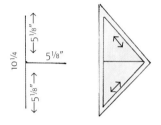

Figuring the triangle

Corners

Border Corners

There are four different ways you can join the corners when you are adding borders—straight corners, block corners, butted corners, and mitered corners. Your decision will depend on your fabric and the look of your quilt. Whichever corners you choose, you will want to make sure all the borders are the same length to keep the quilt square.

To calculate the length of the borders, measure all four sides of your quilt and average the numbers. If your quilt is rectangular, make sure you use the correct border length on the two long sides and the two short sides.

Straight Corners

When you add borders for straight corners, cut borders for the quilt's two smaller sides first. The borders should be the same

Flowers in Appliqué

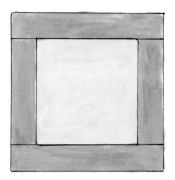

Straight corners

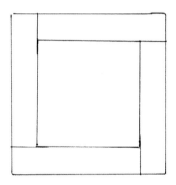

Block corners

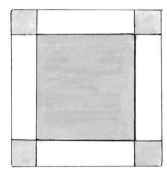

Butted corners

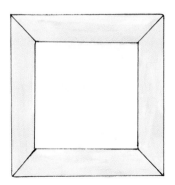

Mitered corners

length as that side of your quilt top and whatever width you desire, plus a seam allowance. Fold the borders in half lengthwise to find their center, and mark the center of each with a pin. Now find the center of your quilt top and pin the center of your border to the center of your quilt. Pin the two ends of the borders to the ends of the quilt, and then add additional pins in between, about every 5″ (12.5cm). Attach the second border to the opposite side in the same manner. Then sew the borders in place.

Next measure the other two sides to determine the length of their borders, and find their center. Pin and sew as discussed earlier.

Block Corners

Block corners usually are designed using two different fabrics, one for the block itself and another for either side of the block. If your quilt top is square, measure all four sides (and average the sides if there is any difference) to come up with the length of each border. Then cut four pieces of fabric the length of the border and the width you desire, adding ½″ (1.3cm) seam allowance to each. Cut four square blocks for the corners, using the width of your borders as the measurement for your squares.

Find the center of one side of your quilt and pin it to the center of one of your borders. Pin the ends together next and add additional pins about every 5″ (12.5cm). Sew together.

Sew one block to the end of the next border and press. Find the center of the quilt side and the center of the border, and pin together. Pin the ends next, then pin about every 5″ (12.5cm). Continue with the next side in the same way. On the fourth side, sew the blocks on each end and press. Find the center and continue as above.

Butted Corners

Measure the length of one side to be bordered, and determine the width you want your finished border to be. Add these two measurements plus a ¼″ (0.75cm) seam allowance. If your quilt is square, cut all four borders the same size. If your quilt is rectangular, cut the two shorter borders as described above. Then measure the longer side and cut the other two borders in the same way.

To add the first border to your quilt top, calculate the width of the finished border plus a ¼" (0.75cm) seam allowance. Using that figure, measure in that distance from the end of one border, on the side to be attached to the quilt. Place a pin there as your starting point, and pin the rest of that border to the quilt, right sides together. Stitch the border to the quilt, using a ¼" (0.75cm) seam allowance. The next border will butt up against the border you have just completed. Pin the second border to the end of the first border with right sides together. Keep sewing along the second side of the quilt, again using a ¼" (0.75cm) seam allowance. Continue on to the third and fourth borders in the same way. When you've finished sewing on all four borders, stitch the first border's corner to the last border's end.

Mitered Corners

Mitered corners are useful when adding whole strips of fabric for borders. If the borders are cut accurately so the design is the same in every border, your eye will continue around the border. Taking careful measurement of the quilt and figuring the length of your borders will allow you to determine how the corners will look.

To determine the length of the border to be mitered, measure the length of the quilt. Add to that the width of the border times two. Then add 1½" to 2" (4cm to 5cm) to be sure you have enough fabric to work with. In other words, border length = quilt length + (2 × border width) + 2" (5cm).

When you have cut the width of your borders, fold one in half and measure from the center to your determined border length. Check what will be in the mitered corner. With a slight adjustment you may be able to have a flower in the corner, or something else that might carry your eye around the corner. Take your time choosing what will be in the corners. Press the center fold.

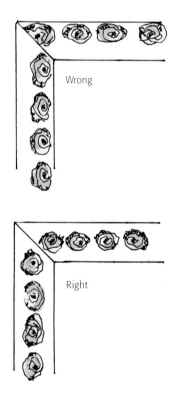

Mitered corners

Flowers in Appliqué

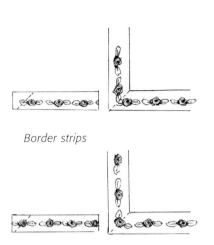

Border strips

Better choice for corner

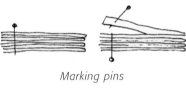

Marking pins

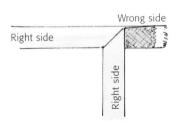

Center fold ↑

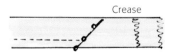

Making mitered corner

Sewing mitered corner

Technique: Keeping the Quilt Square

By following these directions and by having all the borders the exact same length, you can ease or slightly stretch the quilt to fit the borders.

Take your border strips, fold them in half, and lay them on top of one another with all the folds at one end. Measure all four sides of your quilt top and average the lengths if they are not the same. Divide that average by two. Using that figure, measure from the folds and push a pin through all the layers, ¼" (0.75cm) in from the edge. Carefully turn the pile over with the pin through all the layers. Place a pin on each border as you pull it off where the original pin was. These will be your marking pins.

Pinning the Borders

Lay your quilt inside these pins and place pins ¼" (0.75cm) inside the edge of the quilt. You will start sewing and stop sewing at these pins. Pin at the center and then about every 4" to 5" (10cm to 12.5cm) to hold in place. Sew starting ¼" (0.75cm) in from the edge, and backstitch. Repeat on the other three sides. Make sure not to catch the previously sewn border strips.

Making Mitered Corners

At the ironing board, press the left-hand border flat from the top so that the seam is pressed toward the center. Turn the quilt over so the right side is up and the left-hand border lies along the length of the ironing board. Make sure the adjoining border is at right angles to the left-hand border. Lay the excess of the second border strip on top and parallel with the left-hand border with right sides together. With your finger gently fold in the right angle. If it does not go easily, check to see if you have started ¼" (0.75cm) from the edge in both directions. Press in the right angle. Pin the border ends so they do not shift.

Lift up the top border and pin along the fold line. Sew from the outside edge down the crease line, just to where the stitch lines come together, and backstitch. Be sure not to catch other fabric in the corner or you'll get a pucker.

Creating a Floral Medallion Quilt

Simple Treasure
Making a Medallion Quilt

You will make Blue Rose, a 78" × 78" (198cm × 198cm) quilt. Medallion quilts can vary greatly since there are no set sizes for the center or the borders. I enjoy designing the medallion center, but beyond that the fabrics themselves seem to tell me how they should be used: the smaller patterns for patchwork, medium-size fabrics for the borders, and larger florals for appliqué.

One thing I especially like about making a medallion quilt is that it's easy to change your mind when you're sewing together a border. I might have the whole quilt planned out before I start, but as the quilt grows from the center, other ideas emerge as I complete each border.

Instructions

1. Cut two 12" (30cm) squares from your ground fabric for the center medallion and the stuffed-work backing.

2. Using your large-floral fabric, select one large flower with leaves for the medallion's center. Cut out the printed motif, leaving 3/16" (0.5cm) seam allowance all around. Position motif in the center of your 12" (30cm) square block of ground fabric. Attach the motif to the fabric with the glue stick. Appliqué as in Chapter 1.

3. Using a light box, trace a feather design around your printed motif. Layer the medallion block (facing up), 12" (30cm) square polyester batt, and 12" (30.cm) square backing. Place them in your quilting hoop and quilt the feathers. Remove from the hoop, turn to the back side of the medallion, and trim the backing and batt from the feathers with appliqué scissors.

4. Cut your 5" (12cm) wide border fabric into four strips, each 12" (30cm) long. Sew the border strips to your corner blocks, as described earlier in this chapter. Then attach your borders to your center block. You have now made your first border.

5. Cut four 8" (20cm) wide strips that are 45" (114cm) long from your monochromatic fabric. Add these strips to your center, using the instructions for applying borders with mitered corners. These strips are now your second border.

6. Lightly draw a grid that is 2½" (6.3cm) square on your monochromatic second border.

7. Using the medium-floral fabric designated for the outer border, cut four 8½" × 86" (21.6cm × 218cm) strips. Set aside the rest of this fabric for your pumpkinseeds.

SUPPLIES

3¾ yards (3.4 meters) white or off-white ground fabric

3 yards (2.75 meters) large-floral fabric for center medallion and garland border (your choice of colors)

48" (122cm) of a complementary 5" (12cm) wide border fabric

Four contrasting 5" (12.5cm) squares for border's block corners

1 yard (0.9 meter) light monochromatic medium-floral fabric for pumpkinseed ground

3½ yards (3 meters) medium-floral fabric for pumpkinseeds and outer border (darker than your center)

1 yard (0.9 meter) dark medium-floral fabric for border-edging design and binding

2½ yards (2.3 meters) quilt-backing fabric, 108" (274cm) wide

Double bed–size cotton batt

Washable glue stick

12" (30cm) square polyester
   batt for feather stuffing in
   center medallion

Appliqué scissors

Freezer paper for
   pumpkinseeds and
   border-edging design

Feather design

8. Using the pattern provided, cut 35 pumpkinseeds from your freezer paper (enough pumpkinseeds to complete one side of the second border). Iron the freezer paper onto your pumpkinseed fabric, leaving ¼" (0.75cm) all around every seed. Cut seeds out with about ¼" (0.75cm) seam allowance. Lay the seeds diagonally on the border, as shown, and glue them onto the fabric with the washable glue stick. Leave the freezer paper on to show you where to turn under your appliqué. (The stiffness of the freezer paper also makes the fabric easier to handle.) Appliqué the pumpkinseeds to the border. You can then remove and reuse the freezer paper patterns on each of the other three sides of the border. Continue as you did on the first side, appliquéing all the pumpkinseeds in place.

9. For the third border, cut four strips 11½" × 65" (29cm × 165cm) from your ground fabric. From your border-edging fabric cut 12 strips that measure 1½" (4cm) × the width of your fabric probably 45" (114cm). Use one strip for each of the four inner border-edging designs. Then sew together two more strips for each of the four outside border-edging designs. Lay the inside border-edging strips along the inside of the ground fabric, right sides facing in the same direction as the quilt. Treat the border-edging strip and the ground as one piece of fabric. Sew them to the center medallion as described earlier in this chapter in the section on keeping your quilt square.

10. Miter the corners of the ground fabric, leaving the border strips free at the corner seam for now.

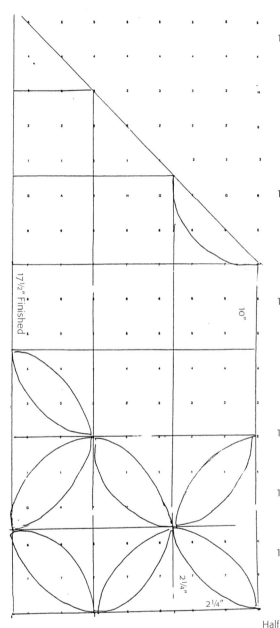

17½" Finished

10"

2¼"

2¼"

Half

Grid for pumpkinseed

11. Cut a freezer-paper pattern using a template made from the border-edging design. The pattern should be the same length as the inside measurement of your border. Iron the freezer-paper pattern onto one of the inside border-edging strips and appliqué the border-edging strip to the border. Remove the freezer paper and reuse it in the same way for the other three sides of this border.

12. Machine-baste the outside border-edging design to the edge of the border. Cut additional freezer paper or reuse your freezer-paper pattern for this outside edge. Again, you can reuse this pattern on each side. See Chapter 5.

13. Cut a garland from your large-floral fabric as described in Chapter 2. If your overall floral fabric does not have a natural garland, create your own garland using a bias strip or by arranging the large florals you selected in a unique and balanced way. Use the glue stick to apply your garland to the ground and then appliqué.

14. Using the medium-floral fabric for the outer border, sew the borders to the quilt and miter the corners as shown earlier in this chapter.

15. Layer the quilt backing, batt, and quilt top, as shown in Chapter 9. Quilt as desired, by hand or machine.

16. Bind the quilt using 2" (5cm) strips of the dark medium-floral fabric you used in the border-edging design

Creating a Floral Medallion Quilt

seven

Creating a Floral Block Quilt

When you use printed motifs in a block-style quilt, you are actually creating many small floral pictures. You have the opportunity of arranging these pictures however you choose. The arrangement you select becomes your quilt. You can use many different fabrics in a block-style quilt; some of the background fabrics will be cut away and only the flowers will show. Block-style quilts allow you to try out the many flower-arranging techniques discussed in Chapter 4.

Floral blocks with printed motifs make a wonderful choice for a group quilt. Start by finding a fabric that you might use to border all the blocks, or choose a fabric that will be used as sashing between the blocks. Everyone can share in finding printed motifs to go with the border or sashing. Each quilter will enjoy the fun of designing her own block. The finished quilt is sure to be unique.

Summer Flowers, 68″ × 68″ (173cm × 173cm)
Designed and hand-stuffed by Judy Severson,
machine-quilted by Shirley Greenhoe

Printed-Motif Blocks

You can fill some of the blocks with flowers using printed motifs from several fabrics. Or you can create blocks from a single fabric. Select one group of flowers, and cut out two, four, or six of the same group. Try arranging them using the kaleidoscope technique, as in *Summer Flowers* (first row, center) on page 94. Experiment by combining some flowers with a light monotone fabric, as in the first block in the second row. You might create small arrangements in the center of a single block, but you can also create two smaller arrangements in opposite corners of one block, as in the top right-hand block.

Perhaps you could appliqué a bow from some other fabric onto a single group of flowers (see *Summer Flowers*) or create bouquets with flowers from different fabrics that you've used in other blocks. When you repeat flowers from one block to another, it has a unifying effect on your quilt.

This quilt was made almost spontaneously over the course of a few days. I started out using flower motifs from previous quilts and arranging them in a few blocks. It was exciting to try different combinations of these flowers in a new arrangement in each block. I had such fun making the blocks with flowers, I made two extra before I realized I already had enough for the quilt. I made this quilt to fold over the back of a chair or to arrange at the end of the bed. On a cold winter afternoon, I like to curl up under a quilt that is filled with summer flowers.

Creating a Floral Block Quilt

You might also combine butterflies, birds, and other motifs from nature with your flowers. Think about using toiles, with their many romantic scenes, as a motif to appliqué in a block. You can select one large scene and appliqué it all together, or you can choose several small scenes and combine them to fill a block. You can add other floral motifs to a toile. You can even encircle a special scene with a wreath of flowers.

Alternating with Floral Fabrics

You can use blocks of a single floral fabric alternating with the printed-motif blocks. You might have one floral fabric too wonderful to cut up, so use it, as is, as a whole block. If you have such a fabric, start with that and select the printed motifs to go along with the fabric or to accentuate the colors in the fabric. Also, you might try to appliqué some of the flowers for use as a printed motif.

If you have a toile fabric, it too might be used as a whole piece of fabric in alternating blocks. Center different scenes in the middle of the alternating blocks.

Alternating with Patchwork

Simple patchwork using large-floral prints makes a good block to alternate with printed-motif blocks. *Evening Star, Ohio Star,* and other star variations also make lovely alternating blocks. Try other smaller patchwork blocks, like *Nine-patch* or *Irish Chain,* made up of smaller floral prints, to blend with alternating printed-motif blocks.

Alternating with Quilting

Other ideas for alternating blocks include quilted feather wreaths, quilted bouquets, flowers, hearts, birds, or butterflies. You might take these designs from the printed motifs by using the outline of the flowers as a quilting pattern in the alternating blocks. All the blocks can have the same quilting design, like a feather wreath, or each block can be different. You can also fill the blocks with background quilting to allow more space between the motif blocks.

Larger Central-Motif Blocks

Some quilters make block-style quilts with one central block of printed motifs that is two or three times larger than all the other blocks, as in *Evening Star* on page vi. The central block is often surrounded with other blocks, each designed with printed motifs. This idea was popular in the nineteenth century when album quilts were made for someone special, such as a minister, a bride, or a family member who was moving away. The large central block gave room to say something personal to the recipient of the quilt. The other blocks were then signed by the friends giving the quilt. This was especially popular when India ink was introduced, since it was the first permanent ink.

Mostly Patchwork

Evening Star was made up of blocks of patchwork alternating with fabric blocks, with a large center of a printed-motif bouquet. Other popular patchwork patterns, such as *Delectable Mountains*, *Little Sawtooth*, and *Rocky Glen*, have been used at times to surround a center filled with printed motifs. What these patchwork patterns have in common is that they are simple triangles in different sizes, they contain only one other fabric, and they use some of the ground from the printed motifs. Patchwork patterns are subtle and do not take away from the printed motifs; the colors actually enhance the overall quilt.

Square or On Point

Once you decide how to fill each of your blocks, consider whether you will use the blocks square or on point. This decision will help you in designing your printed-motif blocks. For example, you can then determine the direction of a bouquet in a block.

If you choose to have all your blocks on point, all the blocks will be the same size, but you will need to figure the size of the triangles by the edge or border of your quilt. In Chapter 6 we discussed how to figure the size of a triangle when a block is on point.

Sashing

Sashing refers to the strips of fabric that separate the blocks from each other. With sashing each block of the quilt is framed. The decision whether to use sashing should be carefully thought out. Not all block-style quilts need it.

Generally, if you use sashing with printed-motif blocks, you should use a continuous sashing. This means that the same fabric frames every block, which helps to unify all of the blocks. However, if you want to introduce another fabric at the intersections between blocks, it is called sashing with squares. You might choose sashing with squares if you feel the quilt needs another color in the corner of the frames around the blocks.

If you decide to use sashing, your next choice is whether to use it only between the blocks or between the border and the blocks as well.

When figuring the amount of fabric you need to buy for sashing, figure in the width of the sashing that will go between each block as well as the width of the blocks. If the sashing is 3″ (7.5cm) wide, then there will be a 3″ addition to each block that you will need to allow yardage for. Always assume the fabric is 40″ (101.5cm) wide rather than the stated 44″ to 45″ (112cm to 114cm) printed on the bolt of fabric. It is better to have extra fabric than to be short.

Technique: Sewing the Blocks Together with Sashing

Lay out all the blocks on a flat surface, leaving room for your sashing. Decide on the width of the sashing between your blocks, and cut the sashing fabric to that width, adding ½″ (1.3cm) for seam allowance — ¼″ (0.75cm) on each side.

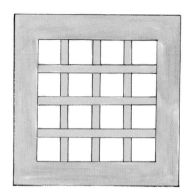

Continous sashing within border

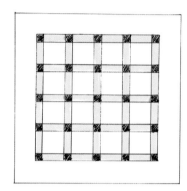

Sashing with squares around all the blocks

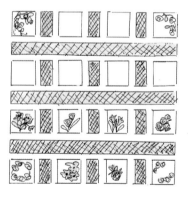

Continuous sashing

Flowers in Appliqué

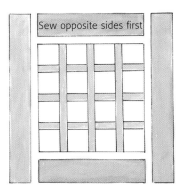

Sashing all around

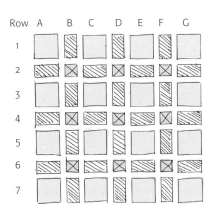

Sashing with blocks

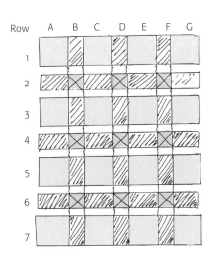

Chaining sashing with blocks

Continuous Sashing

For continuous sashing, cut the sashing the same length as your block, including the seam allowance, and lay the strips vertically between each block. Figure the length of the horizontal sashing by multiplying the number of blocks times their width. Add that figure to the measurement of the sashing between each block. It is always better to cut it longer than to have to piece it.

Sew all the vertical blocks together with the sashing as you have it laid out. Press the seams to one side. Sew the horizontal sashing strips and press.

If you wish to add the same sashing all around, sew two strips on opposite sides the length of the completed blocks. Press the seams to one side. Cut two more strips the same length, adding the width of the two outside sashing pieces. Sew to the remaining two sides and press. You can also miter the corners if you wish as described in Chapter 5.

Sashing with Blocks

Cut the sashing strips the length of your unfinished quilt block, including seam allowance. Lay the strips between the quilt blocks. The width of the sashing will dictate the size of your sashing blocks. Cut the fabric for the sashing blocks into squares and lay them into place.

Sew row 1 with right sides together, using a ¼" (0.75cm) seam allowance. Sew A to B. Do not lift the needle after stitching across the block. Start row 2 and sew A to B. Do not cut the rows apart. Continue to the next row, leaving the thread between the blocks. When you get to the last row, cut the thread.

Then start again with row 1 and sew B to C, again not lifting the needle. Sew row 2, B to C, and continue down the row. Continue across the quilt. Press the seams to one side.

You will then have all the blocks chained together. Sew the rows together using a ¼" (0.75cm) seam allowance.

Simple Treasure
Making a Floral Block Quilt

You will make Summer Flowers, a 76" × 76" (193cm × 193cm) quilt. When you start making a block-style quilt with your printed motifs, choose fabrics for your border, sashing, and printed motifs that will blend well together. Don't be afraid to add fabrics that contain a few brighter tones to add sparkle to the quilt. One way I have done this is by adding a blue bow to a group of flowers. I gave the bow added dimension, or depth, by first sewing the bow to a fabric that will provide its shadow. Then I sewed the bow in place on the block. The ground fabric might be a light calico print or a tone-on-tone white or off-white fabric that will add texture to the background of your quilt. Let all the colors marinate as discussed in Chapter 3.

Instructions

1. Cut four strips 6″ × 47″ (15cm × 119cm) from your ground fabric and set it aside for the feather border. Then cut nine 10½″ (26.5cm) square blocks from your ground fabric for your printed motifs.

2. Arrange printed motifs as shown in Chapter 4, and appliqué into place.

3. Use freezer paper to trace the pattern for a bow, and then cut out the pattern. Center the pattern on your bow fabric and iron it on using the cotton setting.

4. Lay the bow fabric on top of the shadow fabric and safety-pin around the bow on the wrong side of the fabric.

5. Appliqué the bow to its shadow by cutting away the bow fabric a few inches ahead of where you are stitching. Needle-turn your fabric under the pattern and appliqué.

6. Cut shadow fabric to ½″ (1.3cm) larger than bow and appliqué it onto a bouquet that has been appliquéd to a block.

7. Add additional embroidery to the blocks if you wish.

8. Look at the basic shapes in each block—circular, square, or directional—and arrange the blocks so they balance each other. The extra time you spend arranging the blocks will make the whole quilt more interesting.

9. Cut sashing fabric into strips 1″ (2.5cm) wide, adding ¼″ (0.75cm) on each side for seam allowance, for a total of 1½″ (4cm), and the same length as the border fabric. Sew the blocks together as shown earlier in this chapter.

Supplies

- 1⅓ yards (1.2 meters) ground fabric
- 1⅓ yards (1.2 meters) large-floral fabric for border edging and printed motifs
- ½ yard (0.5 meter) pieces of five different medium- and large-floral fabrics for printed motifs
- 6″ (15cm) square of fabric for bow
- 6″ (15cm) square of fabric for bow's shadow
- 2¼ yards (2.1 meters) sashing fabric
- 2¼ yards (2.1 meters) border fabric
- 4½ yards (4 meters) backing fabric
- Twin-size cotton batt
- Craft-size medium-loft polyester for stuffing feathers
- Freezer paper
- Safety pins
- Embroidery thread (optional)

10. Cut border-edging floral fabric into strips 1¾" (4.4cm) wide (including seam allowance) and the entire length of the fabric.

11. Lay the border-edging strip along the edge of the ground for the feather border. Have both fabrics facing in the same direction and treat them as one. Sew the border onto the blocks. Miter the corners as shown in Chapter 6, but leave the border edging free from miter.

12. Cut the border-edging pattern and appliqué as shown in Chapter 5.

13. Add sashing strips and border as shown in Chapter 6.

14. Draw feathers and stuff them. Complete as shown in Chapter 9.

The bow pattern

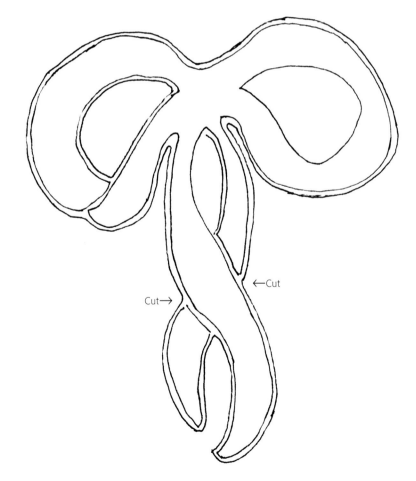

Cut→

←Cut

eight

Creating a Floral Framed Quilt

floral framed quilt designed in a classic style is one of the most romantic quilts. By classic style I mean with a balance to the placement of the printed motifs and other appliqué, reflecting almost a rhythm in its design.

These quilts remind me of May Day as a child, dancing with colorful ribbons around the May pole with flower wreaths in our hair and tossing small roses from our pockets as we danced. Or of throwing a bouquet of flowers into a pond and watching the larger flowers remain grouped together in the middle, while waves of smaller flowers float out from the center.

I have collected more than 20 pictures of framed chintz quilts dating from about 1800. I found myself longing to make one. But where was I to begin placing flowers on an expanse of off-white ground the size of my bed? Once I found a fabric that just seemed perfect for this style of quilt, I found myself dividing up the quilt into rings and then into smaller sections. I then made *Belvedere Garden* (see page 122). After I finished, I realized just how easily these quilts can be made. They start from the center, whether as a single rose or a large basket of flowers, and have rings that flow outward.

Ring of Roses, 88″ × 88″ (224cm × 224cm)
Designed and hand-appliquéd by Judy Severson,
machine-quilted by Shirley Greenhoe

You can create the rings in four different ways, and they can be used in any combination with each other. The rings can be made up of any combination of printed motifs, conventional appliqué, feathers, or other quilting designs. When you have decided how you want to create the rings, you can then place them in position by dividing up the quilt like a piece of pie. Then you can add more printed motifs, other appliqué, and quilting along the edge of the quilt before you add the border.

The Center

The center of your quilt should be one of your prettiest flowers or a group of flowers. Whatever you use in the center, it is a good idea to use some of those same flowers in another ring, in the four corners of your quilt, or somewhere they can be repeated to give the quilt continuity. These flowers should be what inspired you to make this quilt.

When I found these beautiful roses in a neutral-color fabric, I knew they would be perfect in a monochromatic printed-motif quilt. It did not matter to me that there were no other fabrics with printed motifs. I felt that I could make this quilt if I could find a few other fabrics that blended no matter what their designs. Starting with my fabrics at home, I found the calico for the double-vine ring and the small check that would later become the swag edging. I succeeded in finding the remaining fabrics on a visit to my quilt store. At this point I made a list of the possibilities for what the rings could be in a framed quilt. Looking at the fabrics themselves helped me eliminate some of the ideas. The rest of the quilt seemed to come together in a matter of a few months of working only in the evenings.

Creating a Floral Framed Quilt

You can try any of the flower-arranging techniques from Chapter 4 to find the best center. Always consider several alternatives before making your final selection.

Single Rings

The most obvious design choice for one of the rings is a single circle of flowers. These flowers may be cut out individually and appliquéd close together or placed in groups at intervals around a circle. Another possibility for a single circle is a circle of feathers. Or you might use other quilted flowers in a ring. Look at the flowers in the center and see if they might make a nice design for a pattern of stuffed quilting in a ring around the center.

Try making a ring of patchwork stars that you then appliqué. Patchwork stars with four, six, or eight points, or even small compass stars, can add color to a floral framed quilt.

Undulating Rings

A second type of ring for a floral framed quilt is an undulating design. This is a ring that floats rhythmically from one side to another around a circle. You might fill this ring with printed motifs, a line of leaves, or a quilted feather cable or flowers.

Place this ring far enough away from the center to undulate several times and show off its design.

Double Rings

Creating a ring with intertwined vines or cables around the center makes a marvelous double ring. You can also design a double ring that is made up of one or more floral motifs, a vine of calico leaves, or a quilted cable and feather ring. I chose a simple twisted vine with ivy picked from my garden for the first ring shown in *Ring of Roses* (see page 106).

Single circle of flowers · Groups of flowers in a circle

Feather circle

Stars in a single ring

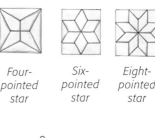

Four-pointed star · Six-pointed star · Eight-pointed star

Leaves · Printed motifs

Feathers

Undulating rings

Flower and leaves ring · Double vine · Cables and feather

Flowers in Appliqué

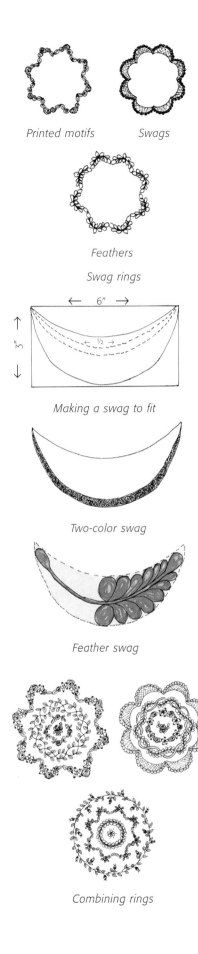

Printed motifs　　　Swags

Feathers

Swag rings

← 6″ →

3″

← ½ →

Making a swag to fit

Two-color swag

Feather swag

Combining rings

Swag Rings

You can design a swag that is made up of individual printed flowers or groups of flowers. I selected a group of flowers for *Ring of Roses* using the instructions in Chapter 2. However, the groups of flowers, like the swag shown in Chapter 9, were actually parts of circles joined top and bottom in a continuous large stripe.

You can make swags using one fabric or two. These swags are easy to create and very effective. Generally, they are twice as long as they are wide from the top of the swag to the bottom. The width of the swag then is more or less half the entire length of the swag. You can easily design swags to fit any circle. Choose from solid, calico, check, or practically any other fabric. Attach the swag with the freezer-paper method. Then appliqué using a slip stitch while needle-turning.

Swags of feathers make a fitting ring for a floral framed quilt. Draw the feathers to fit in a swag as described. In Chapter 9 I will show you how to draw your own feathers.

Your fabrics almost suggest the type of ring that you should make. For example, the fabric I used in the swag ring in *Ring of Roses* blended with my motifs (although when I bought the fabric I was not sure what I was going to do with it). Since it was a plaid, I knew I would use it as a swag or a ribbon, wherever I decided to include it.

Combining Rings

You can make up any number of rings depending on the size of your framed quilt, the size of the center, and how deep or thick the ring or rings will be. One to four rings generally will fill the quilt.

Squaring Off

You can add motifs such as bouquets of flowers, all the same or different, along the quilt edge before you add a border. Groups of flowers soften the quilt's edge when moving from the rings to the square border. You may also wish to add a border-edging design to accomplish the same thing.

Fill your corners with a single flower or basket of flowers before you add your border. Try adding birds or butterflies either from printed motifs or made from a pattern. Feathers or other quilting designs are another option.

Technique: Designing Rings

Designing rings is much the same as designing borders (see Chapter 5). The only difference is that there are no corners to contend with. Draw the rings on pattern paper first. You can make half the pattern on a single piece of pattern paper, or you can tape two pieces together to draw the large center part of your quilt. Once you've designed your rings, transfer the pattern by using a light box or cutting out the pattern and laying it on the ground fabric. Then draw around the pattern onto your ground fabric.

Single Rings

You can draw a single ring by using a compass if the ring is smaller than 12″ (30cm). If you need a larger circle, you can make your own pattern by creating a paper compass. Here's how: Lay a long piece of clear tape over the inch (cm) marks on your pattern paper. I usually use a piece of tape that's ¾″ × 28″ (2cm × 71cm). Cut around the tape to create a paper ruler (the clear tape gives the paper more stability while allowing you to read the measurements). Using a hole punch, make a hole at the 1″ (2.5cm) mark at one end of the paper ruler. Then decide the approximate size of the circle you want to draw. For this example, let's create a circle that is 20″ (51cm) in diameter. Punch a second hole on the inch (cm) mark that is 10″ (25cm) away from the first hole. Lay out a piece of pattern paper large enough to draw your circle on. Now insert a pencil through the first hole you punched. Hold the paper ruler over your pattern paper with the pencil in the center. This pencil will be the center of your compass and will be the pivot point for drawing your circle. Next, insert a second pencil in the second hole at the 10″ (25cm) mark on your paper ruler. You'll use this second

Clear tape over pattern paper

Flowers in Appliqué

Undulating ring

Double ring

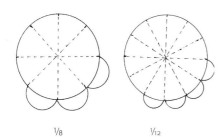

1/8   1/12

*Stitching lines for center
of framed quilt*

pencil to draw your actual circle. Hold the paper ruler so it lies flat on the pattern paper and hold the drawing pencil perpendicular to the paper. Keeping the paper ruler flat and using light tension, move your paper ruler in a circle around your pivot pencil, drawing as you go.

You can adjust these instructions to create any circle you want, by punching additional holes at 1″ (2.5cm) intervals for your drawing pencil. This gives you the flexibility to try drawing circles that are either larger or smaller than the size you originally planned. Using your paper compass also works well for drawing half-circles. I find this helpful when my paper isn't big enough for the whole circle.

Undulating Rings

To make an undulating ring, start by drawing a single circle of the size you need on pattern paper. On a piece of scratch paper, draw a circle the width of your undulate—3″ to 6″ (7.5cm to 15cm) in diameter. Cut out about 12 more paper circles the same size. Lay the circles around the ring and space them evenly. You will need an even number to go around the ring. Connect the circles by drawing a line that weaves from the inside of one circle to the outside of the adjacent circle to create an undulating ring.

If you want more undulation, add more circles. If you want a thicker or thinner ring, adjust the size of the circles.

Double Rings

The double ring is made by first following the directions for an undulating ring. Next, add a second line, using the other side of the circles.

Swag Rings

Draw a circle the size of the space where the swags will meet. Divide the circle into eight, twelve, or sixteen sections like a pie. The easiest way to divide the circle is to fold the pattern paper into the number of swags you want. Then draw the swags as discussed.

Creating a Floral Framed Quilt

Simple Treasure
Making a Floral Framed Quilt

You will make Ring of Roses, an 88" × 88" (224cm × 224cm) quilt. First choose all of your fabrics for this quilt. Select one or more fabrics to use for your border. Then decide on the completed size of your quilt. Subtract the border size from the completed size of the quilt to figure the size of the large center.

The large center of a framed quilt is larger than the width of fabric. You will need to sew two pieces together or add two pieces on either side of the center. Because the center is so large and you are holding a lot of fabric when you appliqué, you can make this quilt in sections if you wish. When making a quilt in sections, you have to be very precise when you design each section and when you put it together after it is appliquéd. However, I find that there is less anxiety when I make it as one piece. It is not any more difficult to appliqué, but there is more of it.

Instructions

1. Using pattern paper, draw half of the large center of the quilt—35" × 70" (89cm × 178cm)—on the pattern paper. Draw lines marking half the quilt and a line from the outside corner to the center.

2. Using your paper compass (described in the section on how to make a single ring, page 110), place pencils 7" (18cm) apart. Draw a 14" (35.5cm) circle. Draw two more circles with pencils 13" and 25" (33cm and 63.5cm) apart for the outer rings.

3. Place your center flower on the pattern paper and draw around what would be the outside edge.

4. Use the pattern to lay on your innermost circle. If you wish to design your own leaf pattern, use 3" (7.5cm) circles and design a double ring as described on page 111.

5. To make the second ring, arrange floral motifs in small garlands around the ring as described in Chapter 2. Adjust your motifs until they are evenly balanced.

6. To make the third ring, combine the motifs and calico ivy with swags made of two fabrics. Sixteen swags make up the ring. Use the pattern provided to draw on the pattern paper or draw your own as described.

7. Cut ground fabric in half and sew together either in halves or thirds.

8. Using an iron, fold your quilt top into eighths and press the fold lines into the fabric.

9. Center the printed motif on the ground, and attach with a glue stick. Appliqué using the needle-turning technique.

Supplies

- 4 yards (3.6 meters) off-white fabric (ground)
- 2½ yards (2.3 meters) border fabric
- 1½ yards (1.4 meters) printed-motif fabric
- 1 yard (0.9 meter) calico for the leaves
- 1 yard (0.9 meter) swag fabric
- 1 yard (0.9 meter) swag-edging fabric
- 2 yards (1.9 meters) border-edging fabric
- 2 yards (1.9 meters) pattern paper
- Freezer paper
- Safety pins
- Washable glue stick
- Template plastic
- Paper compass (see "Designing Rings," page 110)
- Double bed–size batt
- 3½ yards (3.1 meters) backing fabric, 108" (274.3cm) wide

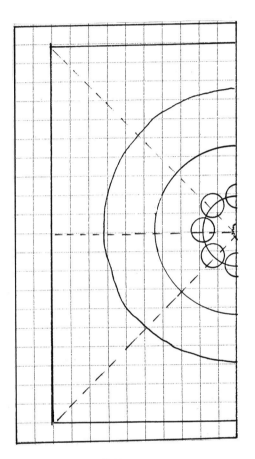

Pattern paper
Drafting a pattern

10. Create a 25″ (63.5cm) square piece of freezer paper by ironing two pieces together. Center the freezer paper on the pattern paper and trace the design. Cut out freezer paper (it can be folded into eighths to cut several layers at the same time). Cut a 25″ (63.5cm) square from the calico. Press lines into eighths. Center freezer paper on the calico and press freezer-paper pattern onto calico.

11. Center the calico on the ground. Using safety pins on the underside, pin all around and in the center to hold in place. Pins should be about 3″ (7.5cm) apart. You may use a glue stick if you prefer. Starting with the outside leaves, trim calico, leaving ¼″ (0.75cm) beyond the freezer paper. Cut 3″ to 4″ (7.5cm to 10cm) ahead as you appliqué. Needle-turn the calico onto the ground. Next move to the inside leaves before completing the leaves in the center of the vine. Be careful not to cut the ground when trimming the calico.

12. Using your paper compass, draw a circle with a pencil to make a second ring, which is 26″ (66cm) in diameter. Arrange your motifs on the ground fabric, using the glue stick. Appliqué using the needle-turning technique.

13. Cut 16 patterns for swag top and edging, using freezer paper. Iron freezer paper onto the swag fabric leaving ¼″ (0.75cm) all around, and cut out leaving ³⁄₁₆″ (0.5cm) seam allowance. Using safety pins on the wrong side, pin one swag top to the swag-edging fabric through the freezer paper in two places (or use the glue stick instead of pins if you prefer). Appliqué the lower edge of the swag. Press the edging pattern onto the lower edge of swag and cut the lower edge ³⁄₁₆″ (0.5cm) beyond freezer paper. Trim off the edging to ¼″ (0.75cm) from the underside of the swag top. Continue making the swags.

Creating a Floral Framed Quilt

14. Cut 16 swag drops and edging from the freezer paper. Sew the top and edging as in step 13.

15. Using your paper compass, draw your third ring, placing pencils 25″ (63.5cm) apart. Lay your swag drops every 7″ (18cm) around the third ring. Make sure they are evenly balanced all around. Use a glue stick on the swag drops to hold them in place. Appliqué, using needle-turning technique.

16. Place swag between drops and use the glue stick to hold it in place. Needle-turn to appliqué.

17. Cut two separate freezer-paper patterns for the calico leaf spray. Iron onto the calico. Using safety pins on the wrong side, pin in place (or use the glue stick). Check to make sure your flower motif will cover the stems. Appliqué as usual.

18. Cut out 16 flower motifs for the top of the swag, leaving $3/16$″ (0.5cm) seam allowance. Place the flower motifs over the stems and the top of the swag, then hold them in place with the glue stick. Appliqué them onto the ground.

19. Cut four strips 2¾″ (7cm) wide from your border-edging fabric. Place one strip facing up on the outside edge of your large center. Machine-baste. Then machine-baste the other three as shown in Chapter 6. Cut one unit of border-edging design out of template plastic. Draw the pattern on freezer paper as shown in Chapter 5. Cut out and iron on the outside edge of the border-edging fabric. Appliqué as usual.

20. Cut four borders 11½″ (29.2cm) wide from your border fabric. Sew the borders on, using the directions in Chapter 6. Apply borders with mitered corners and keep the quilt square.

21. Complete your quilt with batt, backing, and quilting (see Chapter 9).

Flowers in Appliqué

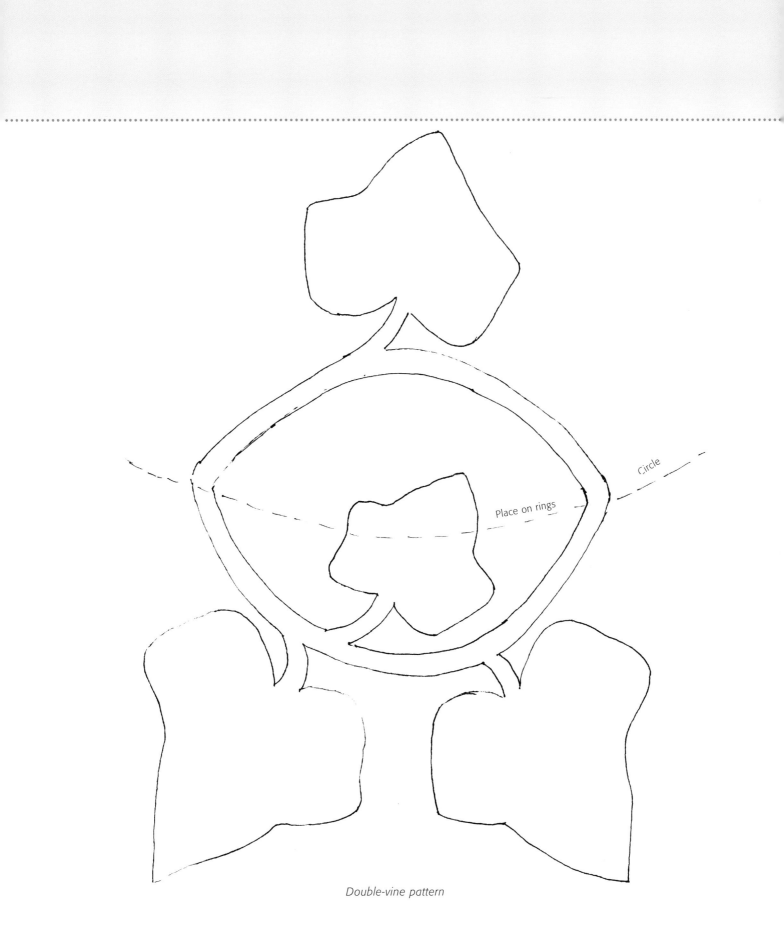

Double-vine pattern

Creating a Floral Framed Quilt

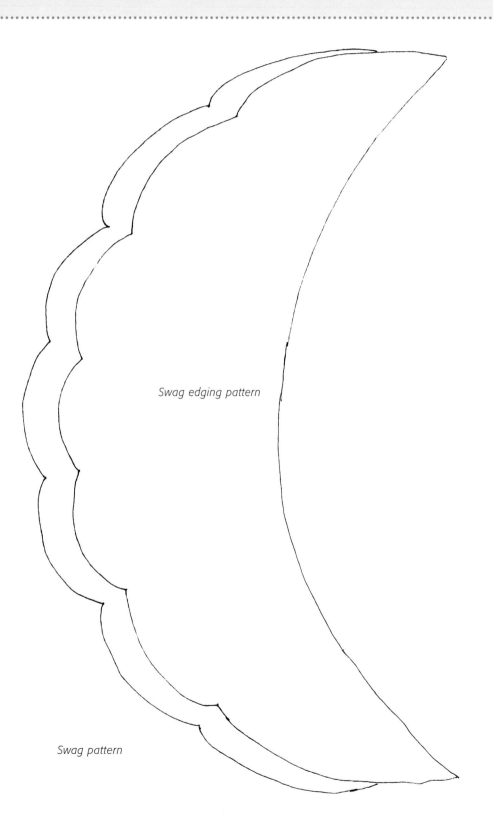

Swag edging pattern

Swag pattern

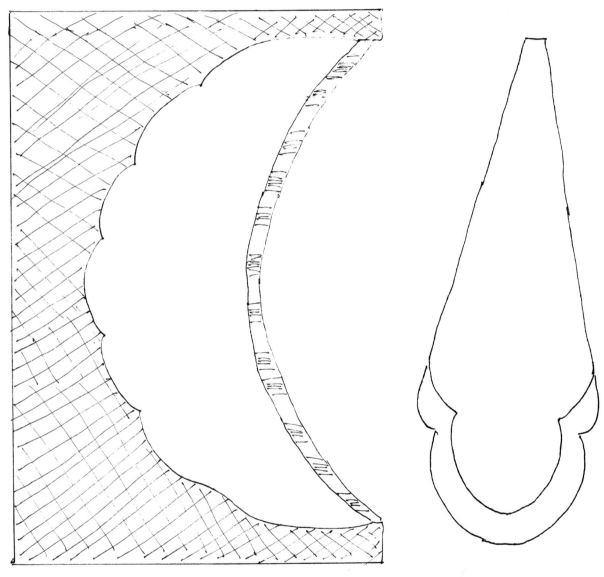

Freezer paper and swag top appliquéd to swag edging

Swag drop pattern

nine

Embellishing Stitches, Stuffed Work, and Quilting

Embellishing Stitches

In many cases, you can use embellishing stitches to appliqué rather than the usual tack stitch. Or you may wish to add embellishing stitches as pure decoration. The herringbone was the stitch most commonly used in the early chintz quilts, according to Averil Colby (*Patchwork Quilts*, 1965). Quilters of that time traditionally used white thread to cover the raw edges after they tacked their floral motifs in place. Blanket or buttonhole stitches were also popular and were frequently stitched with colored silk thread to emphasize the outline of the motif. You may also use other embellishments, such as the chain stitch, to cover the raw edges of a printed motif. Or try the outline stitch in place of the tack stitch when you turn the raw edges under. Consider using colored or metallic thread for your stitches.

The satin stitch may be used to adorn many of the simple treasures described in this book. Silk or metallic threads will add extra richness to these small projects. You may also want to add French knots or beads to the center of a flower to make it more eye-catching. Feather stitching works well with printed motifs. I used this stitch on the pincushion on page 68.

Belvedere Garden, 90″ × 90″ (229cm × 229cm)
Designed and hand-appliquéd by Judy Severson,
hand-quilted by Toni Fisher

Herringbone, buttonhole, or chain stitch

Herringbone stitch   Blanket stitch

Buttonhole stitch   Chain stitch   Outline stitch

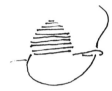

Satin stitch   French knot   Feather stitch

Stitches used in place of tack stitch

*his is the first frame-style quilt **I** made. **E**ven though the large size made it bulky to appliqué, the quilt went together easily and quickly. **I** made the top over a three-month period using any free moments **I** could find. **T**he quilt is named for the city where **I** live, which was celebrating its centennial. **I**n the romance language **I**talian, belvedere means "terrace," usually overlooking a landscape or other engaging view.*

Adding embellishing stitches and stuffed work to a quilt before it is quilted will make it extra special. These details enrich any floral-motif project and are well worth the time they take. Along with the quilting design, they help make a quilt uniquely your own.

Stuffed Work

Stuffing is an extra layer of quilting that you add under feathers or flowers to give them an added dimension. Stuffed work is actually done before the quilt is quilted. By doing the stuffed work before you quilt, your work is less likely to become overstuffed, which would result in a misshapen quilt.

I recommend a medium polyester batt and thin backing for your stuffed work. Use a quilting hoop that is a few inches larger than the image you are stuffing. If you are stuffing a continuous feather, let the feather extend across the hoop. Layer the quilt top, polyester batt, and backing. Safety-pin around your image on the wrong side. Place it in the hoop with the image facing up, and quilt your image. If you are creating a continuous feather and you need to add additional batt or backing, lay the extra piece so it is just touching the piece already in place. You do not want to make additional thickness by overlapping the extra materials. Then trim out the backing and the batt, leaving the feathers or flowers raised.

Stuffed work should only be done on white or very light-colored fabrics for best effect. Otherwise, none of your painstaking work will show up. One of my students found this out the hard way after doing stuffed work on a gray fabric, which barely showed her beautiful feathers after many hours of labor.

Wrong side of quilt top

Trim away with appliqué scissors. Back and batt as closely as possible.

Stuffed work

Hand-Quilting Essentials

If you decide to hand-quilt your work, use a needle called a "between," number 10 or number 12. The larger the number, the smaller the needle when you are hand-quilting. Tie a knot in your quilting thread as discussed in Chapter 1. Starting about 1″ (2.5cm) from your quilt line, insert your needle down into the quilt top only. Bring the needle back up on your quilt line. Pull up on the thread and give it a jerk to pull the knot through the top. The knot should catch in the batting.

You will want your quilting stitches to be as even and as small as possible. The more you quilt, the better your stitches will become. Position the needle at a right angle from the quilt, close to

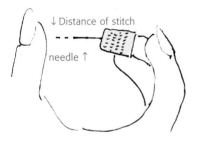

↓Distance of stitch

needle ↑

Quilting

where it came up, and push the needle straight down through all the layers. You will feel the needle point touch your fingers beneath the quilt backing. Use a thimble to rock the needle down and up away from you horizontally to sew several stitches on the needle. The amount of needle showing above the quilt will be the length of each stitch.

When you have used most of the thread and are ready to tie off, wrap the thread around the needle. Slide the loop close to the quilt top and tighten the knot. To hide the knot, insert the needle one stitch ahead and come out ½" (1.3cm) ahead. Jerk the needle, pulling the knot inside with the batt. Trim the thread.

Hand-Quilting Designs

There are many plastic quilting stencils available today. You might use these in addition to or in place of your background quilting. It is also easy to make your own quilting stencil using template plastic. For instance, you might have used a printed motif that you would like to repeat as a quilt design, adding to the individuality of your quilt. Simplify the image by just outlining it on tracing paper. Then use a light box to transfer the image onto your quilt, marking lightly with a silver marker or a pencil.

Feathers make an ideal hand-quilting design when you use them with printed motifs. Their curved lines are organic and lively. They are also easy to draw if you know the basics. Since there is more than one type of feather, you can vary the style of the feathers as well. I'll show you several different feather designs later in this chapter.

Background-Quilting Designs

After deciding on your overall quilting pattern, you may want to fill in with background quilting. The quilts from the past offer many different ideas for your background quilting. For instance, you can stitch parallel lines of quilting or grid quilting in any widths. These two background-quilting designs remain popular today.

Clamshell, double parallel lines, and double grids also create a pleasant texture as background-quilting designs.

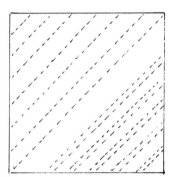

Parallel lines; double parallel lines

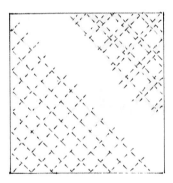

Cross-hatching or grid; double grid

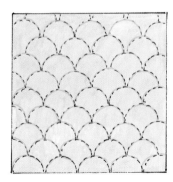

Clamshell

Background Quilting

Echo quilting around printed motifs allows you to continue the feeling of your appliqué. You can achieve this by quilting around the shape of the appliqué using lines that are equidistant from each other.

Stippling is very tight quilting that meanders. It is like echo quilting but the stitches are much closer and they lend a different texture to the ground. Stippling next to stuffed work makes it look puffier.

You can draw any of these quilting designs on your quilt using a silver marker or a pencil and marking lightly. It is easier to mark the quilt before you baste it together with the batt and backing.

Echo quilting

Stippling

Layering the Quilt: Putting It All Together

Press out wrinkles before marking, checking that all seam allowances are flat. Fold the quilt in quarters with the right side folded in. Once you have chosen your quilting design and marked it on your quilt top, you are ready to put it all together. To prepare the quilt top for quilting, trim off any loose threads that show on top.

The quilt backing and batt need to be 4″ (10cm) larger overall than the quilt top. The backing should be wrinkle-free and any loose threads should be trimmed. The material you use for the batt is a matter of personal choice. I prefer an all-cotton batt.

Use a large table or work on the floor to lay out the backing right side down. Make sure it is smooth. Use masking tape or tablecloth clamps to hold it tight. Then center the batt on top of the backing and spread it out smoothly. Find the center of the batt and lay the quartered quilt top in place. Open up the top and smooth it out. Make sure all layers are flat.

Baste the three layers together, starting in the center and working to the outside. You can use a grid pattern, basting every 4″ to 6″ (10cm to 15cm), or a radiating pattern. Use a long thin needle such as a number 7 sharp.

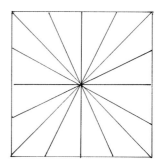

Basting—Grid

Basting—Radiating

Flowers in Appliqué

Frames and Hoops

You may choose from a variety of quilt frames and hoops. A 10″ (25cm) hoop for smaller projects and a 14″ (35.5cm) hoop for larger projects are good sizes to begin with. Plastic frames are easy to adjust, lightweight, and great for traveling. Large frames vary, so get good advice before buying. Some quilters do beautiful work without frames or hoops. The advantage of a hoop or frame is that it will keep your surface smooth for quilting. The tension of the quilt does not need to be tight. You will begin stitching in the middle of your quilt and work outward.

Machine Quilting

Having your quilt machine-quilted is another option. You can do this yourself or hire a professional. Half of the quilts in this book were professionally machine-quilted at a reasonable price. This is becoming a very popular trade, so the prices should remain favorable. You will have many different styles of quilting designs from which to choose, and the designs can vary throughout the quilt. Before you choose a machine quilter, though, be sure to check out the quality of his or her work.

Binding

The binding is the material that covers the raw edges of your quilt and gives it durability. I recommend a French binding, which is a double-thickness. You can create your binding from the same fabric you use in your outermost border, or you may choose a different fabric to complement or contrast with your other fabrics.

Your binding needs to be 2″ to 2½″ (5cm to 6.3cm) wide for ¼″ to ⅜″ (0.75cm to 1cm) binding, and about 4″ (10cm) longer than the distance around all four sides of your quilt. I generally prefer small bindings. You probably will have to cut several pieces of fabric and join them together to bind the entire quilt. Before cutting the binding, however, test the width of the binding by folding it in half on the edge of your quilt. This way you can be sure the bind-

ing is wide enough to wrap around the edge and still have a ¼"
(0.75cm) seam allowance on each side. Cut the binding on the
straight grain of your fabric.

When joining strips of binding, layer the right sides together,
placing them perpendicular to each other. Machine-stitch a diagonal seam and trim the seam to ¼" (0.75cm). Press seam to one
side. When you have a few more inches of your binding sewn
together, fold the binding in half with right sides out and press.

Binding Corners

Start in the middle of one side of your quilt. Follow the instructions
above for folding your binding, and lay the folded binding on top
of your quilt top. The raw edges of the binding should be lined up
with the outside edge of the quilt, and the quilt should be right side
up. Begin sewing 1" (2.5cm) from the end of the binding and stop
¼" (0.75cm) from the corner using a ¼" (0.75cm) seam allowance.
Backstitch at the corner. Place a pin in the binding at the corner of
the quilt, making sure the pin is only in the binding and not in the
quilt itself. Place a second pin ¼" (0.75cm) from the first pin in the
extra binding that extends beyond the quilt edge.

Fold the binding perpendicular to your stitch line so that your
first pin marks the edge of the quilt and the second pin is above.
This will create a mitered corner. Next, fold the binding down,
making sure that the first pin stays in place and that your second
pin is now on top of the just-completed row of stitching. Secure the
binding to the quilt at this point, and begin by backstitching at
your second pin. Continue stitching along the next side of the quilt,
stopping ¼" (0.75cm) from the corner. Backstitch to hold securely.
Continue around the quilt, stopping 2" (5cm) away from where you
started.

Binding Finish

To finish the binding, take the beginning of the binding strip and
fold its end inside itself ½" (1.3cm). Lay the binding end inside the
folded binding strip. Trim away the excess binding to ½" (1.3cm)
beyond the beginning fold. Pin to the quilt and finish stitching the
binding.

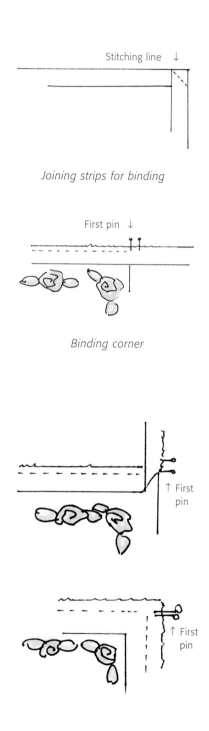

Stitching line ↓

Joining strips for binding

First pin ↓

Binding corner

↑ First pin

↑ First pin

Flowers in Appliqué

Fold the binding to the back of your quilt and slip-stitch the folded edge of the binding to the back.

Technique: Designing Feathers to Fit

I had the good fortune to take a class on drafting feathers several years ago from a wonderful teacher named Lucy Hilty. I now call all my feather quilting "Lucy's feathers." However, I learned more from Lucy than just how to draw my own feather designs. Lucy's brilliant idea of using circles to make feathers flow around a border has become a basic tool in all my quilt designing. For I soon realized that her technique for drawing feathers could also be used to design any continuous border pattern, from vines to ropes to garlands. I explain Lucy's method in detail in Chapter 5.

Over the years I have seen a variety of feathers, from short and round to long and graceful, from small and dainty to large and grand. Since there are many different feathers to put in a quilt, feathers should vary with the quilt you are making. Lucy's technique allows you to adjust your feathers to your own quilt, rather than using someone else's ready-made pattern.

Drawing Feathers

Using scratch paper, draw three parallel lines 2" (5cm) apart and about 12" (30cm) long. The center line will be the starting point for your feathers, which will extend out from there to the outer lines on either side. Some quilters like to work from a double center line. If you wish to do so, draw another set of parallel lines on either side of the center line. Make those additional lines ¼" (0.75cm) from the center line.

Decide which direction you want your feathers to go. Using the feathers in the illustration on the next page as an example, practice drawing your own feathers. Some quilters like to draw feathers by always starting from the center line. Others prefer to draw their feathers on the right-hand side starting from the center line, but create the left-hand feathers by starting on the outside line and drawing in to the center line. Try playing with different techniques and see what works best for you.

Experiment with your feather shapes too, but keep the following in mind: the top of the feathers should always be rounded. Some people like to use coins to make them round. Feathers ought to have a continuous curve, so there should be no straight lines in your feathers. Most important, the top of each feather should be at a point that is directly opposite from its starting point. This will ensure that your feathers have the most pleasing shape possible.

As you study feathers in other quilts, you'll see that the ones from older quilts were usually longer and more sensuous, while today many are shorter and rounder. Remember, a feather is like a signature, so draw your feathers until you find one you like best.

Once you are comfortable drawing your own feathers, you are ready to mark your quilt. You can draw your feathers freehand directly onto your quilt using a silver marker or light pencil. Or, if you prefer, you can make a plastic template of a single feather to use as a pattern.

If you decide to use a template, draw a double line on your quilt for the center, and then lightly draw the outside lines. Now use your single feather template to draw each feather in between. Just draw the outside edge between one feather and the next. Then fill in freehand the soft curve of the feather from the center out.

Undulating Feathers

Undulating feathers are started the same way as a straight line of feathers. Draw your center line (or lines) and the accompanying outside lines. But instead of drawing straight lines, your lines will continuously curve around your quilt. Chapter 5 tells you how to draw lines for undulating vines; undulating feathers are created in the same manner.

Design a feather and use it as a template. Place the template so it touches your center line. Mark the placement for the tops of your feathers only. Remember that the top of each feather should be at a point directly opposite from where you started it at the base. You can then fill in your feathers from the center line to where the feathers are touching each other. Note the way the feathers fan out

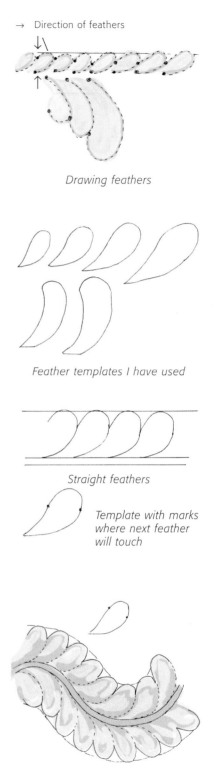

→ Direction of feathers

Drawing feathers

Feather templates I have used

Straight feathers

Template with marks where next feather will touch

Undulating feathers

Flowers in Appliqué

and move. Again, be sure there are no straight parts on the feathers. Each feather should always tuck into the previous feather.

Feather Wreaths

Making the feathers into a circle is a bit of a challenge. Work this out on paper first because there is always a certain amount of adjustment that you will have to make. This time draw your center line in the shape of a circle. Add the two accompanying outside lines. Draw a few feathers with your template, placing a mark to show where you will line up the next feather. After you draw your feathers halfway around the circle, check to see how the rest of the feathers will fit by placing a dot where each remaining feather will be. If it looks like you will have too much space, add more room between the feathers. If you end up with a space that is too small for a whole feather, move the other feathers a little closer together to make room for your last one.

Once you have the tops drawn in with the template, hand-draw the rest of the feathers. Start at the center line, across from where the feather joins the last feather. Let your line follow the circle first, then continue drawing in a curve up and out toward the touching feathers.

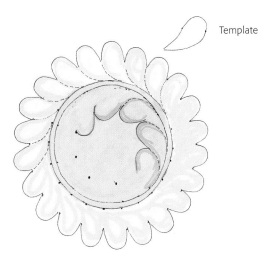

Template

Feather wreaths

Simple Treasure
Table Runner with Feathers

You will make a table runner measuring 12″ × 32″ (30cm × 81.3cm). Runners under china, silver, and glass seem to make these objects more elegant. I love using them throughout the house but particularly in the dining room. This feather runner was inspired by the china bowl that sometimes sits on my dining room table. The bowl has an interesting family history. It was passed down to our family from a New England sea captain, who plied the England–China trade routes during the early nineteenth century. The bowl has blue and gold feathers that wind their way around the piece while they intertwine with each other.

Instructions

1. Cut the following from your white fabric:

    Two rectangles 9½" × 29½" (24cm × 75cm) for the feather top and lining

    Two rectangles 9" × 12" (23cm × 30cm) for the feather lining at each end of the runner

    Two strips 1½" × 13" (4cm × 33cm) for the border-edging design

    Two strips 1½" × 34" (4cm × 86cm) for the border-edging design

2. Using a light box, trace the feather pattern onto one of the larger white rectangles. Center your floral motif on the feathers you have drawn onto the rectangle. Attach the motif, using webbing or glue stick, and then appliqué.

3. Layer a cotton batt and a 9" × 12" (23cm × 30cm) rectangle under the rectangle with the feathers. Pin with safety pins on the underside around the feathers.

4. Place in a quilting hoop and quilt your feathers. On the reverse side of the runner, cut out the lining fabric and batt from around the feathers with appliqué scissors.

5. Place the feather top, facing up, on top of the 9½" × 29½" (24cm × 75cm) white lining. Using your sewing machine, position your needle ¼" (0.75cm) from the edge and baste the two pieces together.

6. Cut the following from your contrasting fabric:

    One rectangle 12½" × 32½" (31.7cm × 82.5cm)

    Two strips 2½" × 45" (6.3cm × 114cm) or width of fabric

    Two strips 2½" × 13" (6.3cm × 33cm)

7. Place one white border-edging strip—1½" × 13" (4cm × 33cm)—on top of contrasting fabric border strip—2½" × 13" (6.3cm × 33cm)—with the long edges flush on one side. Sew the border-edging strip and con-

Supplies

1 yard (0.9 meter) white or light-colored fabric

½ yard (0.5 meter) contrasting fabric

2 printed motifs

Webbing or glue stick for appliquéing motifs

Two pieces of 2" × 12" (5cm × 30cm) cotton batt

Safety pins

Quilting hoop

Appliqué scissors

Small piece of template plastic

Freezer paper

Flowers in Appliqué

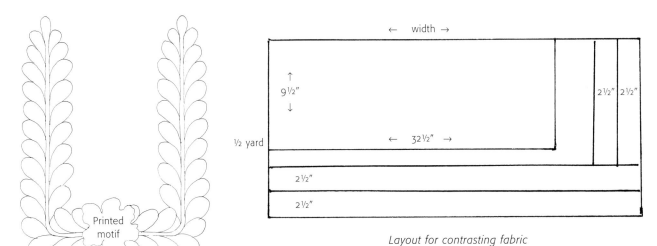

Feathers for runner

Layout for contrasting fabric

*Border-edging design for runner.
Use white or off-white*

trasting fabric onto one end of the feather center. Sew on the other end the same way. Layer the 1½" × 34" (4cm × 86.4cm) white border edging on top of the contrasting 2½" × 45" (6.3cm × 114cm) strip and sew to the sides of the feather center. Keeping the white border-edging separate from the contrasting fabric, miter the corner of the contrasting fabric as described in Chapter 6. The miter does not have to go all the way into the feather center because the border-edging design will cover half of the contrasting border.

8. Trace the pattern for a single border-edging unit and transfer to template plastic. Cut out the template. Use the template to draw your border onto freezer paper for the border-edging design. You will need seven units for each end of the runner and 20 units for each side of the runner. Press the freezer paper onto white border edging and sew as directed in Chapter 5.

9. Place your completed runner top with contrasting lining right sides together and pin to hold in place. Sew together using a ¼" (0.75cm) seam allowance, starting along the long side. Continue sewing around the runner, leaving a 5" (12.5cm) opening at the end. Reverse to the right side. Press and hand-stitch the opening closed.

Quilt Patterns

Printed motifs

Conventional appliqué

Floral fabric

Patchwork

Quilting and stuffed work

*A*ll printed motifs combine well with appliqué, patchwork, fabric borders, and quilting, both plain and stuffed. In the patterns that follow, I have used symbols to represent each of these different quilting techniques to make it easier for you to find your way to techniques of special interest to you. For instance, if you have a fabric that goes well with your printed motifs, you might want to use it as a fabric border or as part of a patchwork border.

Evening Star and Bouquet

102" × 110" (259cm × 279.4cm)

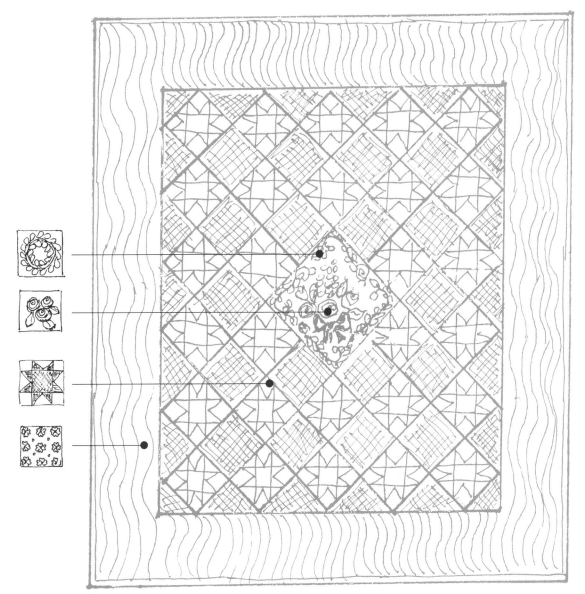

Vintage Rose

65″ × 72″ (165cm × 182.9cm)

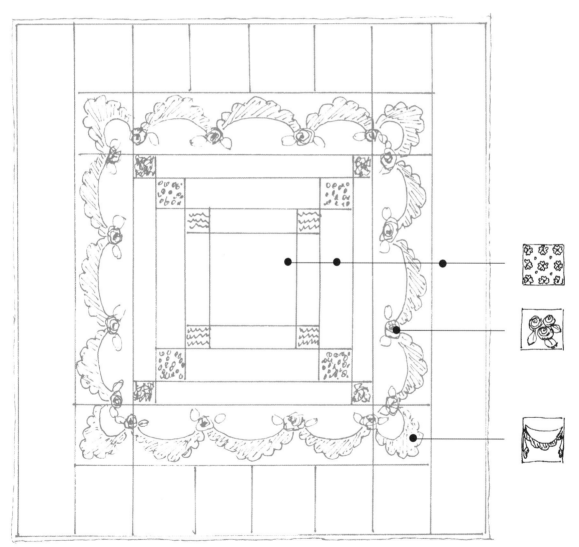

Flowers in Appliqué

Blue Garland

92″ × 92″ (233.7cm × 233.7cm)

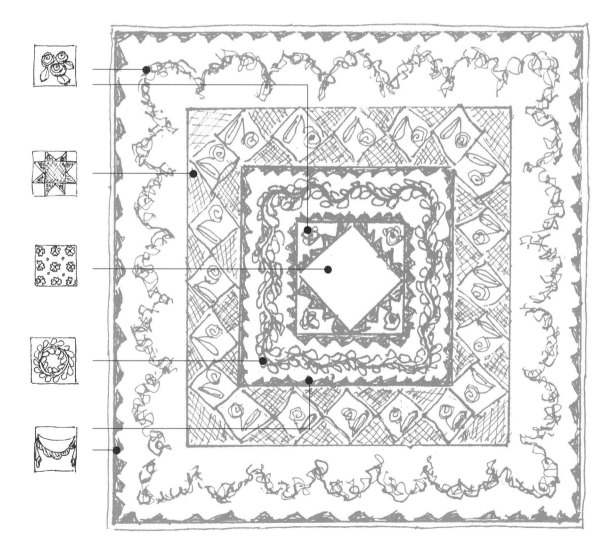

Rose Wreath

94″ × 93″ (239cm × 236cm)

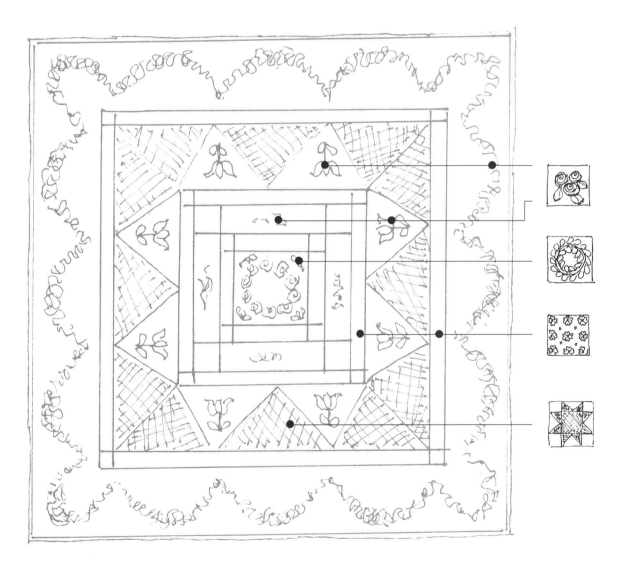

Flowers in Appliqué

Flowers A-Bloom

81″ × 81″ (206cm × 206cm)

Angel Quilt

83″ × 83″ (210.8cm × 210.8cm)

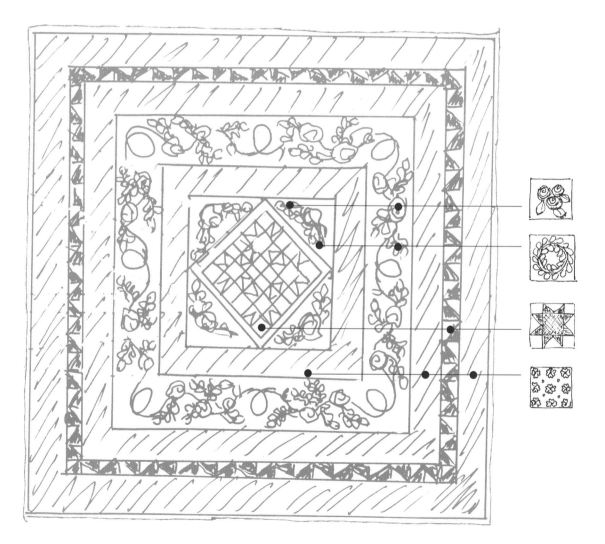

Flowers in Appliqué

Blue Rose

78″ × 78″ (198cm × 198m)

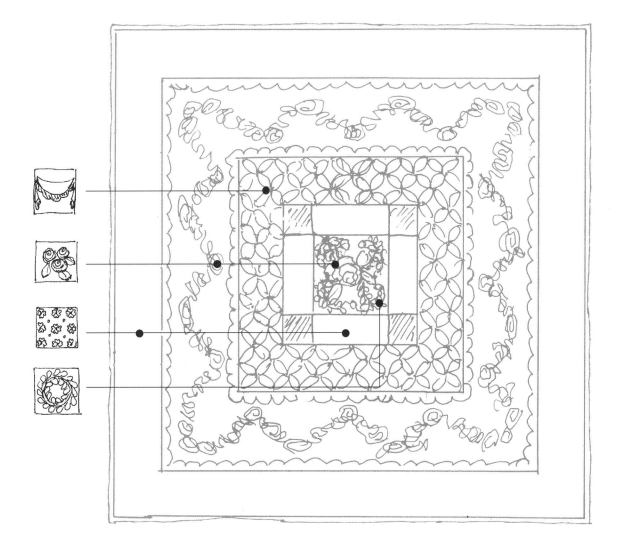

Summer Flowers

68″ × 68″ (172cm × 172cm)

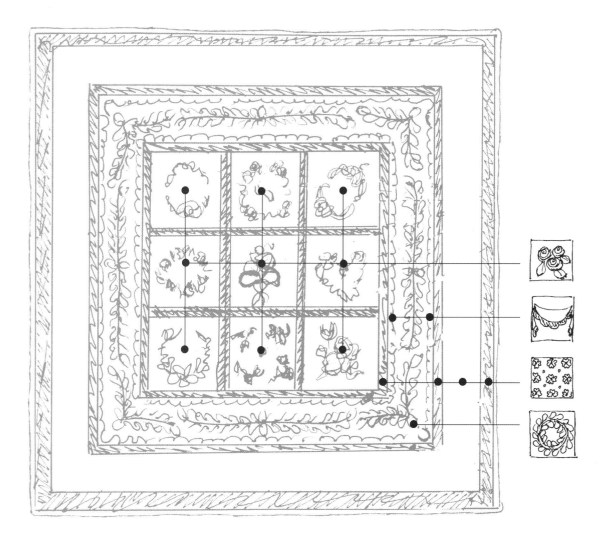

Flowers in Appliqué

Rings of Roses

88″ × 88″ (223.5cm × 223.5cm)

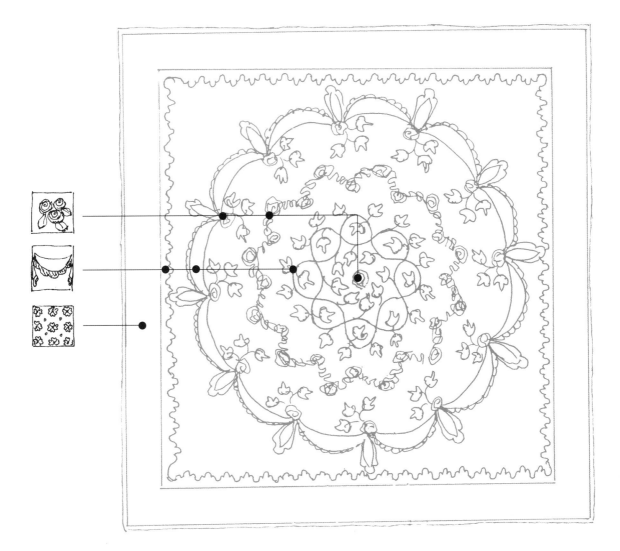

Belvedere Garden

90″ × 90″ (228.6cm × 228.6cm)

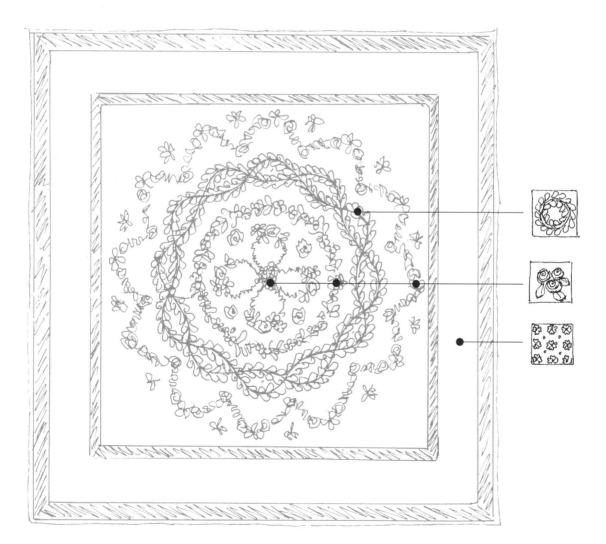

Flowers in Appliqué

Glossary

Appliqué	Small pieces of fabric stitched to a larger piece for a decorative effect.
Background	The background color in fabrics. In this book, the background color in the floral motif.
Backing	The fabric layer on the back or bottom of the quilt.
Batt or batting	The filling between the quilt top and backing.
Block-style quilt	Quilt made up of four or more blocks, sewn together.
Border	Strip or strips around the edges of the quilt top.
Border edging	A continuous piece of fabric that is appliquéd in an interesting way along one edge or both edges of a border. Examples of border-edging designs include dogteeth and curved patterns.
Broderie perse	A French term for Persian embroidery that is encrusted with needlework. Has referred to appliqué cutout since the end of the nineteenth century. It is sometimes still used today as a name for motif quilts.
Calico	A small closely packed pattern printed on fabric.
Chintz	Originally a printed pattern textile, but today a glazed plain or printed fabric.
Chintz quilts	Quilts made of chintz fabrics between 1780 and 1840.
Conventional appliqué	Plain or small-scale fabrics cut into a pattern and appliquéd.
Cutouts	A design or motif that has been cut from one fabric for application to another.
Dogtooth	A type of border edging in which a single piece of fabric is added to a border on one or both sides and cut to look like sharp teeth.
Frame	A single border surrounding a very large central body. Also, fabric added to either or both edges of a border.

Framed quilt	A quilt having a large central body that is made of one piece of fabric (or two pieces sewn together as one) with a single border framing it.
Ground	The fabric to which floral motifs or other appliqué designs are stitched.
Layout	Term used by fabric designers to describe the plan of the textile design.
Medallion quilt	A quilt with a focal central block surrounded by borders.
Miter	A corner formed by two pieces of fabric whose edges fit together at a right angle. A technique for joining borders.
Monotone design	Also monochromatic. A design that uses only one color.
Motifs/Printed motifs	The designs in mid- to large-scale fabrics that are cut out from the fabric and appliquéd to a ground.
Packed	Fabric design in which motifs cover the entire background.
Patchwork	The joining of small pieces of fabric to make a larger one.
Quilt	A bedcover composed of a top, filler, and back sandwiched together with small stitches. When used as a verb, the act of sewing through the three layers.
Sashing	Fabric that is between quilt blocks, framing the blocks.
Spaced	Fabric design in which motifs show a good deal of background.
Stuffed work	Stuffing added before a quilt is quilted to add a design in relief.
Toile	A design composed of scenic motifs rendered in dark, fine outlines on a neutral background. Originally Toile de Jouy referred to cloth from Jouy, France.
Trapunto	Stuffing added after a quilt is quilted to create a design in relief.

Flowers in Appliqué

Books for Inspiration

The following are some of the quilting books I've found to be especially helpful and inspirational. They are listed in alphabetical order by title.

The American Quilt, Roderick Kiracofe, Clarkson Potter Publishers, New York, 1993.

American Quilts, Elizabeth Wells Robertson, The Studio Publications, Inc., New York, 1948.

Appliqué! Appliqué!! Appliqué!!!, Laurene Sinema, The Quilt Digest Press, Lincolnwood (Chicago), IL, 1992.

Baltimore Beauties and Beyond, Volume Two, Elly Sienkiewicz, C&T Publishing, Lafayette, CA, 1991.

Broderie Perse, Barbara W. Barber, American Quilter's Society, Paducah, KY, 1997.

Chintz Appliqué Quilts, Ellen Fickling Earnes, University of North Carolina Press, Chapel Hill, 1988.

Chintz Quilts: Unfading Glory, Lacy Folmar Bullard and Betty Jo Shiel, Serendipity Publishers, Tallahassee, FL, 1983.

Clues in the Calico, Barbara Brackman, EPM Publications, Inc., McLean, VA, 1989.

Enduring Grace — Quilts from the Shelburne Museum Collection, Celia Y. Oliver, C&T Publishing, Lafayette, CA, 1997.

First Flowerings—Early Virginia Quilts, Gloria Seaman Allen, DAR Museum, Washington, DC, 1987.

For Purpose and Pleasure, Quilting Together in Nineteenth Century America, Sandi Fox, Rutledge Hill Press, Nashville, TN, 1995.

Forget Me Not: A Gallery of Friendship and Album Quilts, Jane Bentley Kolter, The Main Street Press, Pittstown, NJ, 1985.

Homage to Amanda—Two Hundred Years of American Quilts, Edwin Binney and Gail Binney-Winslow, The Quilt Digest Press, Gualala, CA, 1984.

A Maryland Album: Quiltmaking Traditions 1634–1934, Gloria Seaman Allen and Nancy Gibson Tuckhorn, Rutledge Hill Press, Nashville, TN, 1995.

North Carolina Quilts, North Carolina Quilt Project, The University of North Carolina Press, Chapel Hill and London, 1988.

Old Quilts, Dr. William Rush Dunton, Jr., self-published, Cantonsville, MD, 1946.

Patchwork, Averil Colby, B.T. Batsford Ltd., London, Eleventh Impression, 1981.

The Quilt Digest Press 4, Michael Kile, The Quilt Digest Press, Lincolnwood (Chicago), IL, 1986.

The Quilter's Album of Blocks and Borders, Jinny Beyer, EPM Publications, Inc., McLean, VA, 1980.

Quilts in America, Patsy and Myron Orlofsky, Abbeville Press, Inc., New York, reprint edition, 1992.

Textile Design, Carol Joyce, Watson-Guptill Publishing, New York, 1993.

Traditional British Quilts, Dorothy Osler, B.T. Batsford Ltd., London, 1987.

Lesson Plan 1
Quilting with Printed Motifs

Description: Discover how to find flower garlands and bouquets in your floral fabrics. Learn how to select a printed motif and use it to make a scissors fob.

Purpose: To show how a variety of fabrics can be used to make a printed-motif quilt. Along with teaching how the different large-floral fabrics can be used in a quilt, show photos of antique and contemporary printed-motif quilts to inspire the students.

Hour 1: Talk about the variety of fabrics that can be used and how to select them. Display a fabric sample that includes hidden bouquets and garlands. Show examples of the three styles of quilts that can be created. Look at the photos in the book and discuss the variety of patchwork, stuffed work, and appliqué in each.

Hour 2: Look at the students' fabrics and discuss them with the whole class. Use the file folder to cut out a guide for finding garlands. Look at photos of chintz quilts from the past.

Hour 3: Make a scissors fob.

Note: This class could be used as an introduction for another class on making the three styles of printed-motif quilts—medallion, block, and framed.

SUPPLY LIST FOR STUDENTS

Floral fabric with about 1½" to 2" (4cm to 5cm) flowers

¼ yard (0.25 meter) coordinating fabric

Fusible web (such as Steam-A-Seam)

Compass

Small piece of cotton batt

Embroidery thread, metallic thread, and beads (optional)

Sewing kit with appropriate needles for threads

Manila file folder

Paper scissors

SUPPLY LIST FOR TEACHER

A variety of quilt fabrics that could be used in printed-motif quilts

Handouts: Illustrations of the stitches that could be used in making a scissors fob; pattern for finding hidden garlands

Extra materials as described in student supply list above for students who forget their own

Your copy of *Flowers in Appliqué: Fast and Simple Quilting with Printed Motifs*

Other books containing examples of chintz quilts (see Books for Inspiration)

8½″ × 11″ graph paper

5 feet dressmaker/pattern
    paper

Compass

Pencils

Eraser

2″ × 12″ (5cm × 30cm) or
    larger plastic see-through
    ruler

Paper scissors

Quilt top to put a border on

Fabrics for vine, flowers, leaves,
    and border

Extra materials as mentioned
    above for students who
    forget their own

Extra paper for cutting out
    circles

Quilts and photos of quilts with
    vine borders

Handouts: Examples of
    different border-edging
    designs; illustrations of the
    four different vine corner
    designs

Lesson Plan 2
Fitting Appliqué Borders

Description: Design appliqué borders easily, using my technique to make vines and flowers flow around the corners of a quilt. Learn how to add printed-motif or other appliquéd flowers and leaves to your borders. Master the art of using border-edging designs.

Purpose: Teach how easy it is to design and make one-of-a-kind borders.

Hour 1: Look at the examples of vine borders you and the students brought. Using graph paper, draw a sample of a complete quilt border, including corners. Then create circles with the compass and paper, following the directions in Chapter 5. Use the circles to demonstrate how to make single-vine borders, then double-vine borders. Talk about the four different corner designs. Hand out border-edging designs and discuss them.

Hour 2: Have students use their pattern paper to design a full-size quilt border.

Hours 3–6: Teach how to make a mitered corner and a bias vine. Explore how to unify the whole quilt by using a fabric or design from the body of the quilt and repeating it in the border. Encourage creativity.

Note: This lesson can be divided into two classes, allowing the students time at home to add a border to their quilt and cut out a vine. The second class would then allow the students to baste or glue (with washable glue or glue stick) the entire vine onto the border.